RETURN TO WIGAN PIER

RETURN TO WIGAN PIER

Ted Dakin

ISIS
LARGE PRINT
Oxford

First published in Great Britain 2011
by
ISIS Publishing Ltd.

Published in Large Print 2011 by ISIS Publishing Ltd.,
7 Centremead, Osney Mead, Oxford OX2 0ES
by arrangement with
The Author

British Library Cataloguing in Publication Data
Dakin, Ted.
    Return to Wigan Pier. – Large print ed.
    (Isis reminiscence series)
    1. Dakin, Ted - - Childhood and youth.
    2. Wigan (England) - - Biography.
    3. Wigan (England) - - Social life and customs - -
    20th century.
    4. Large type books.
    I. Title II. Series
    942.7'36082'092–dc22

02116 ISBN 978–0–7531–5269–0 (hb)
       ISBN 978–0–7531–5270–6 (pb)

Printed and bound in Great Britain by
T. J. International Ltd., Padstow, Cornwall

CHAPTER ONE

From Saint To Sinner

In those days, back in the 30s, you could guarantee that the Sunday morning peal of St Joseph's ancient bell would summon enough devout Catholics to fill its ancient pews, and in the front one, nearest to the altar, you would always find the widow, Mabel Meadowsweet and her son, Cyril.

Although almost fanatical in her religious beliefs, Mabel was cold-hearted, detached and uncaring to everyone but Father Gwilliam, his fellow priests and her son, Cyril.

Since the passing of her husband, who she never loved, Cyril and the church dominated her very existence, and she in turn dominated Cyril. Hers was a harsh love that demanded respect and obedience. She, herself, respected no one, except, of course, the young, handsome Father Gwilliam.

When in doubt (which was very seldom) concerning finances, neighbourhood problems and Cyril's upbringing, she relied entirely on the clergyman's wisdom, overwhelming personality and charm. And it was because of his smooth-talking sensibility, Mabel decided that Cyril, too, would become a priest. Yes, there was no doubt about it, Cyril with his impeccable manners, innocent, flawless, angelic looks crowned by a mass of neatly parted blond hair and a soft lisping voice would be the ultimate clergyman. A man of God who everyone would admire and respect. Just like Father Gwilliam, in fact.

Her mind was made up. Father Cyril Meadowsweet, the name, the person, her son, seemed synonymous with the church and religion.

To us, the rascals of Mayflower Road, however, Mabel Meadowsweet's fervent plans for Cyril, were still unknown. To us, Cyril was a mardy-arse, who never played street games (only with the girls), never got dirty and was too clever for his own good. In other words, he was ripe for bullying. Not real thumping stuff — he always seemed too fragile for that — but mussing-up his hair, shoving mud in his ears, tying him to a lamppost and pulling his pants down, and, on hot summer days, daubing his shirt and shoes with sticky tar, seemed to be the right thing to do.

I mean, we weren't asking for much, we just wanted him to join a gang, run wild like us, get into trouble, curse and smoke and play football with a pig's bladder, to live and enjoy life as us kids did in those golden days. Not mope about dressed like a toff, playing girlish games.

Then one day, me and two of my best mates, "Birdy" Briggs, who was always whistling his soddin' head off, and Johnny "Jockey" Johnson, who was as thin as a pencil, cornered Cyril and demanded to know why he was so different from the rest of us.

2

"Mother wants me to be a priest."

A stunned silence followed. Then Birdy began to snigger.

"A bloody priest, are tha bloody kiddin' us or what?"

"And Father Gwilliam thinks so as well."

"You're not old enough, no way," Jockey said.

"I leave school in a few weeks' time, and Father Gwilliam has promised to give me some preliminary private tuition. In fact, Mother and I are in the midst of religious studies even now."

Jockey put on a mocking voice: "Ooh, 'Mother and I', how jolly; tell me, Cyril, if any of the gang committed a sin or uses a swear word . . . I mean, will you absolve us, give us your blessings, like?"

"Don't be silly."

"Ooh," Birdy said. "Don't be silly, Jockey, a boy priest can't do that, not just yet, anyway."

"But what do we call him for now, Birdy?" Jockey said. "Father Meadowsweet, or Saint Cyril?"

Birdy turned to me. "What do you reckon, Eric? What do we call this little sod, eh?"

By this time, I was getting a bit uncomfortable with all this goading; I spat a mouthful of phlegm — tough-like.

"I reckon we should leave off for now." Then, so as not seem too sympathetic, I said, "Let him go running home to his darling mummy and do his studying."

Inevitably, the word spread like wildfire. No one in Mayflower Road, though, would believe such a tale — a priest from Mayflower Road? Never! No one could comprehend such a thing; surely it was made-up. The

3

grown-ups laughed and said it was a figment of Cyril's imagination. But the kids of those grown-ups gave him hell, and Cyril wished and prayed that it would all go away, that it was truly a figment, not of his, but of his mother's imagination.

The stress of all this took its toll, and he broke out in purulent boils that covered his entire back from shoulders to waist. His face, though, still had that cherubic look, making us, the taunters, unaware of his affliction. And time marched on, and we became more tolerable with it all.

Then, in 1939, World War Two broke out. Twelve months later, Cyril received his call-up papers and had to face a medical examination board somewhere in Liverpool. But his mother wasn't worried; they would never take her son, not with the state of that back of his, never. Besides, if there was a hiccup health wise, she would have a quiet word with Father Gwilliam.

Despite Mabel's hopeful expectations, a few weeks later, Cyril, ex-potential clergyman, was dressed in an ill-fitting khaki uniform.

Some said it was because of his domineering mother pleading for his discharge on the grounds of his religious vocation. Some said it was because he just wasn't man enough to stand the rigours of army life. But years later I was told that it was the awful state of Cyril's back, made unbearably painful by his heavy pack and rigorous training standards, that finally broke his spirit.

Whatever the cause, Cyril began to go AWOL, and when he did, which was often, he didn't head for home.

This and several calls from local police to search her house, left Mabel devastated and sick with worry. Where was he? Was he sleeping rough under hedges? Or in some remote and derelict, rat-invested cottage? Or lying dead even in some swollen, turbulent river?

She was nearly out of her mind with worry. Her plans for his future were shattered, but worst of all, he had changed from a church-going, obedient, God-fearing son, who would have excelled as a messenger of The Almighty, giving succour to the poor, the sick and the sinners in these now uncertain times.

She prayed and prayed and sought solace from the soothing, comforting words of Father Gwilliam, who prayed with her for Cyril's return to sanity and stability.

Then, one early morning, an urgent rapping on Mabel's front door awoke her from a troubled sleep. It was Cyril; muddied, bleary-eyed and exhausted, he almost collapsed into her arms.

An hour later, washed, warmed, well-fed and in bed, he was asleep, whilst his doting parent, with the cunning of an over-protective mother, began to plot and plan.

He couldn't stay with her. The police would surely come knocking again. He couldn't return to that horrible army life, not with the war raging out of control. If he was to go back, he would certainly be shipped overseas and come to his end on some muddy foreign field. No, she must think of something. She would protect him, and when the war was over, they would carry on as before. He, a life serving God. She, a life serving him, looking after his every need.

Suddenly, miracle-like, the answer to this conundrum was there, staring her in the face. On the dining table, still strewn with dishes from Cyril's meal, lay the answer: DIG FOR VICTORY. A wartime leaflet issued by the Home Office appealing to the general public to grow their own foodstuff, using lawns, gardens, window boxes and, where possible, borough allotments. That was it! There was still an empty allotment a short distance from Mayflower Road, down by the canal. Its very remoteness had so far detered any would-be growers from moving in. There was even a shed within its confines.

Later that day, a refreshed Cyril sat and listened while his mother told him of her plan.

"But how will I eat and keep warm?"

"I'll bring you food and warm clothes, and there's a Primus stove in the backroom upstairs. You can carry that down there tonight when it goes dark."

Later that day, Mabel left Mayflower Road and took a casual stroll by the canal. The allotment, which lay a few yards back from the water's edge, was overgrown, but luckily the gate was unlocked, and so, too, was the shed, which, considering its situation, was fairly clean and tidy. A further clandestine visit from mother and son, and the place was fit for habitation.

With police visits becoming more and more infrequent, Mabel began to feel confident that her only son had escaped the clutches of the law and a certain gruesome death in battle, although, much to her regret, she knew that priesthood was now out of the question.

She took him clean clothes, food, books and newspapers daily; and it was those newspapers, with pages crammed full of the fighting, the slaughter and the destruction occurring in various parts of the world, even in Britain, and laying to waste the very meaning of civilisation, that finally broke him. He could stand it no longer. One morning, he walked from the allotment, went home to a startled, frightened mother and asked her to accompany him to the police station.

And that spiral down from saint to sinner had been the making of Cyril. He took his punishment, went into combat, fought well and came through unscathed.

And Mabel, forever thankful that her precious son had beaten his demons and had survived the horrors of battle, never really accepted the fact that her son was now a confident, independent young man who had broken the shackles of maternal domination and earned the respect of everyone: Jockey, Birdy, me and the tenants of Mayflower Road. And not forgetting a certain priest whose name was Father Gwilliam, who had most probably prayed and prayed as he had never prayed before to see the end of Mabel Meadowsweet's constant, parental demands.

"Do You Remember?"
A Lifetime Of Memories

"DO YOU REMEMBER?"

Have you read about the latest "Beta Blocker" drug now being developed that could purge bad memories from the brain?

To my way of thinking, memories of any kind, good and bad, are part of life, and the author H. G. Wells gave credence to this when he wrote: "We all live with reference to past experiences, not to future events, however inevitable."

The past is history, and history we cannot live without, and us "owd" folk keep on remembering what used to be — good and bad.

There is hardly a day goes by when I, and others like me, don't talk about those penniless, but simpler times of a bygone age. A time before the unwanted rise of countless bureaucratic officials; a time before the politically correct army and the health and safety brigade began to control many areas of our livelihood and beliefs and, most importantly, that fast-disappearing right to freedom: freedom of speech, freedom of choice and freedom to question what's right and wrong.

Now most people love strawberries, and some folk, on bright sunny days, can't wait to jump in their cars or take a walk to a pick-your-own farm and spend an enjoyable couple of hours doing just that — picking strawberries.

But wait a minute. Is it safe? It could be dangerous, you know. You could prick your finger. You may get stung by a wasp or a bee. But guess what? One gang of health and safety imbeciles down in Cornwall have gone much further than the eradication of a possible bee sting; they have now removed any danger whatsoever lurking among those wicked strawberries, and, to make it official, they have demanded that the owners of one particular farm, who have been in the pick-your-own business for forty years, should install walkways and bridges between each row of strawberries, cordon off potholes and install handrails near open ditches "just in case" of accidents.

The owner (and who can blame him?) has now banned all those once-upon-a-time pickers from an enjoyable, healthy pastime. I reckon those health and safety killjoys deserve a mighty big raspberry from every one of us, don't you?

And what about the arthritic Scotsman (not a joke this) who, on leaving a charity shop, accidentally dropped a £10 note and a receipt which was witnessed by two (yes, two) vigilant coppers, who bravely confronted this arthritic criminal and gave him a £50 fixed-penalty notice for littering the street. It's not often

10

you come across chaps littering our streets with tenners, is it?

Then we have safety in our schools. Children are being forced to wear goggles before handling Blu Tack. Egg boxes have been used for generations to make a variety of playthings; not any more — they have been banned for fear of Salmonella poisoning.

Some schools have banned footballs. Three-legged races have been banned on sports days because it has now been deemed as a dangerous activity.

So how, in this cushioned, cosseted, comfy world can children be taught that physical and emotional knocks in life are an essential and unavoidable part of living?

There was, once upon a time, another world when the majority of Wigan folk didn't have much in the way of money or possessions, and their children, not knowing owt else, accepted this penury and made do with what they had, and they enjoyed a life that was, in many ways, precarious; but they lived it to the full in wild and healthy abandonment.

"DO YOU REMEMBER?"

How sad I feel for the majority of kids today. My upbringing, my world, and, for many like me, life was one continuous adventure, and what made mine so was the location of where I was born and raised. Aye, the bottom end of Miry Lane in the 1930s, 40s and 50s was not a very pleasant place. Not one you bragged about. No way!

We, the tenants of this dead-end Dickensian paradise, were sandwiched between a main railway line, a canal, a foul-smelling boneworks, a busy railway siding and a noisy, dusty brickyard. But what great days they were.

How could anyone with just a modicum of adventure in his body avoid breaking a bone, straining a tendon falling foul of the law (or even worse) in such an environment?

How could we not, in this man-made adventure land, do something we weren't supposed to do? How could we not trespass and "take" a little coal from those sidings for our empty fireplaces?

How could we not enjoy this childhood freedom in a world devoid of televisions, electronic gadgets and all things detrimental to enjoying a wild and wonderful life?

To challenge the girls at spin the bottle (and isn't it funny, we lads never lost a game?) and run and climb and fall and get up to start all over again and again and again. To play street games and swing like young Tarzans from the corner gaslamp.

How could we not share a Wild Woodbine fag and argue and fight and shake hands?

How could we not want to play out in a blistering hot summer sun, popping sticky tar bubbles and getting cursed and a clout from Mam as she smothered you in margarine?

And with all this freedom and activity comes the greatest gift of all: memories. Memories of a time never

12

to be forgotten but never to be repeated: ONLY BY REMEMBERING.

(Note: Since completing this article, I've read that scientists now say that chatting about bygone days can help pensioners boost their brainpower.)

I reckon that us owd uns have known this for years, because we all belong to Winston Churchill's KBO brigade: "KEEP BUGGERING ON."

"DO YOU REMEMBER?"

CHAPTER
TWO

A New Beginning

Except for a battered settee with its two seated occupants, the room was empty. Tom and Frances were waiting for their son, Albert, who had promised to come and collect them in his car, and as usual, Albert was late.

"Where the hell as he got to?" Tom said.

"You know our Bert," Frances said. "He'd be late for his own funeral, besides, he might be giving us the chance to get used to the idea."

"No need for that. We're going whether we want to or not; we're at the mercy of other folk, and that's that."

"Aye," sighed Frances. "We're the last to go. They start pulling them down tomorrow."

"It had to come, Frances; these houses weren't meant to last for ever, you know."

"They could have renovated and left us as we were, all together."

"That's true; whole communities have been uprooted and scattered like bloody seeds."

"It's a crying shame," Frances said. "A crying shame; look at Mrs Blundell and Jim."

"Where is it they've gone to?"

"Why, in one of them high-rise flats t' other side o' town."

"She'll not be doin' any street gossiping among that lot, will she?"

"Not likely. She was a right gossipmonger, that one. It'll kill her off, so it will."

"Aye, she had a tongue on her. She'd cause bother in a convent, that one."

"Do you remember when a gang of the lads were playing football int' street, an' one o' them put ball through her front window?"

"Aye, an' she blamed our Bert . . ."

Frances sniffed. "She never did like our Albert, not since he clobbered their Andrew for kicking our cat."

"And look what happened week after — poor cat was poisoned."

"An' she was a lovely cat, was Tibby . . . it was her that did it; there's no doubt about it."

"Aye, but we could never prove it," Tom said.

"We've had some good neighbours though, Tom; they'd do owt for you."

"That's true. It'll never be the same again."

"We're livin' in a different world, Tom. They're a different breed today . . . By the way, you've still got the bullet, haven't you?"

Tom tapped his coat pocket. "Course I have. After all these years how could I not have it?"

"Our Bert'll be expecting that when you pop your clogs, you know."

"Aye, maybe so, maybe not."

"Course he'll want it. If that Geman sniper had been a little more accurate, there'd be no you, no me and no Bert; that bullet's history, Tom."

"Aye, the war to end all wars, then look what happened; 1939 and another bloody war."

"Thank God our Bert was too young for that lot," Frances said. "And talking about the last one, look what happened to your cousin, Alf."

"Aye, he went through it, poor sod; retreat from Dunkirk, 12 hours up to his bloody neck in water waiting to be picked up, got home, volunteered for the Mercantile Marines and got shipwrecked twice by German U-Boats."

"He were a good swimmer though, weren't he?" Frances said.

"It were a good job he was; he always said he'd spent more time in water than a bloody fish."

There was silence for a while.

"This'll be our first move since 1921, Tom."

Tom smiled. "I remember when we first moved in, day after we got wed, it was. Miss Ballard, our landlady, never did much to make us comfortable, did she? . . . I had to do all the bloody repairs and decorating."

"Anyway, it was ours, wasn't it?"

"Well, sort of, I suppose."

"Put it this way, we did what we wanted with it; we made it ours," Frances said. "And we didn't put airs and graces on like Bertha Boothroyd. She thought she was too good for the likes of us."

"Aye. Her husband were okay though."

"She were that posh, or thought she was, she put her window-bottom figurines and whatnots facing the street, showing off like the person she was . . . my ornaments always faced in. They were there for our pleasure not for the rest o' neighbourhood to gawp at."

"Aye, she liked to show off."

"You're not kiddin'; she were the first one round here to get a newfangled gas oven; anyroad, she came a right cropper with it."

"Why, what happened?"

Frances gave a smug smile. "Why, she bought a tin o' steak in gravy and put it in this 'ere new oven of hers, and the daft sod never pierced the tin. It went off like a bomb . . . blew the oven door open and there were steak and gravy scattered everywhere: ont' walls, units, even ceiling, everywhere."

"Served her right, too, the stuck-up sod," Tom said. "When you think back, Frances, we had a struggle sometimes to keep warm and well-fed, didn't we?"

"At least you never went thievin' coal, not like some round 'ere."

"That's true, but you must admit, those railway sidings and the coal kept plenty folk who had no money to spend nice and warm."

"And kept some in wages too," Frances said.

"I was always tempted," Tom said. "But I didn't fancy dodging railway police and local bobbies just for a bag o' coal."

"Talking about bobbies," Frances said. "Do you remember that swine of a bobbie who used to come round on his bike?"

"Oh, you mean bobbie Welsby."

"That's him, and do you remember that second-hand bike you bought our Albert for his birthday?"

"I do an' all; I bought it off "Knocker" Neill. He used to collect parts from the local tips and do them up — give them a lick o' paint and sell them off cheap."

"That's right, well, one day, while you where at work, that Welsby copper stopped our Bert, right in front of our house and began to give him the third degree, asking him all sorts of questions, he was."

"Like what?"

"Where had he got the bike? How much had it cost? How long had he had it? . . . That sort o' thing."

"The swine!"

"That he was. Anyway, I went out to him and told him to bugger off and leave the lad alone. 'There's a bike been reported missing,' he said, 'I'm only doing my job.' And I told him to bugger off again, and do his job somewhere else."

"And did he?"

"He did."

"But he did have a good side to him," Tom said. "Remember when he pulled that young lad out o' the canal one Saturday afternoon — gave him artificial respiration and saved the lad's life?"

"I remember, but he could still be a swine."

"There's no beat bobbies to be seen these days. If you fall int' cut and you can't swim, you'll bloody well drown."

"Now you mention the canal, Tom, I don't think your mam and dad ever got over givin' up that boat o' theirs, do you?"

"It were progress, as they call it, that did it, Frances, you know, railways and bloody giant wagons; it were them that killed off the canals for being too slow. Pity really, Dad were good for another five years or more."

"Nothing's the same, Tom. Everything and everybody's changing too fast. This little corner of Wigan had a community spirit that'll never be seen again."

"True. We looked after our sick and dying and helped those who wanted help in other ways."

"Do you remember Mr Croston, next door, becoming seriously ill with that abscess?" Frances said.

"How can I ever forget?" Tom said. "We'd just moved in 1921 when the poor bugger had this abscess come on his neck."

"It were on his arm."

"Oh . . . Anyway, Doctor Berry said it had to be hot-poulticed every half-hour because this red line of infection was making its way to his heart."

"That's right; there weren't the same antibiotics like there is today."

"I don't know about that," Tom said. "But that's what Doctor Berry wanted, and you and Mrs Croston sat up all night with him, poulticing and feeding him drinks."

"He pulled through, though, didn't he, Tom, an' Mrs Croston were forever grateful. That's what we did in those days, Tom; it were natural-like . . . she'd a done the same for us."

"Do you know summat, Frances?"

"What's that, Tom?"

"You can be a right secretive bugger when you want to be."

"How do you mean?"

"It's the first time you've mentioned that confrontation you had with bobbie Welsby over our Bert's bike."

"Well, you know now, don't you?"

"But our Bert's 33 years old, woman."

"And I'll tell you another little secret, too."

"Bloody hell, woman, what's this, confessional time without the priest?"

"It's about our Bert again."

"Nothing serious, I hope."

"'Course not."

"Let us have it then."

"Well, one afternoon, I came home from shopping, let myself in the house, and there's our Bert in front of the fire playing with himself."

"You mean . . ."

"You know what I mean; playing with himself."

"And what did you do?"

"What would you have done, Tom?"

"Bloody hell, I don't know."

"Well, I tried to scare him a bit . . . I said, proper stern-like, 'don't you know you'll never be able to see int' dark doing that, mi lad.'"

"And what did he say to that?"

"Well, I thought he'd be all embarrassed being caught out, but all he said was, 'If I save up and buy a torch can I carry on doing it?'"

20

"The cheeky monkey."

Just then, the sound of a car pulling up and the toot of a horn interrupted any more conversation.

"That'll be our Bert come for us," Frances said.

When they went out into the deserted street, Bert had the engine running and both windows down.

"C'mon, you two, let's be havin' you."

Frances stopped at the pavement's edge, and, looking back at the house that had witnessed so much — sadness, tears, sickness and happiness — she knew she had done her very best and made the house what it was: humble, clean and cherished.

She gripped her husband's arm tight. "The end of a way of life, Tom and a new beginning."

"And God preserve us all," said Tom.

"Do You Remember?"
Our House

"DO YOU REMEMBER?"

Recession, recession, recession. Day after day, the message is loud and clear. No one will escape! Money, jobs and essential goods are in short supply.

Once again, the pawn shops are thriving. In a futile attempt to beat this latest doom and gloom downturn, high street shops wave their tantalising SALE signs in a desperate bid to attract custom.

Bricks and mortar, too, are now crumbling before our very eyes, as the housing market is now witnessing what could be the worst property crash since The Great War. FOR SALE signs are removed and replaced by TO LET signs, as the struggle goes on. Young couples wanting a place of their own are in a quandary. To buy or not to buy? To sell or not to sell? What a dilemma.

Now that was one dilemma that the working-class Wiganers of times gone by never had to face; because every house, and I mean every house (where I lived anyway), was landlord owned.

I was born and raised with my two brothers and a sister in the bottom house of Miry Lane, off Wallgate, next door to a foul-smelling boneworks. Can you imagine living next door to a works whose produce was bonemeal fertiliser, glue and sausage skins, all derived from farm animals. In those days the intestines (rops) from slaughtered pigs were used for sausage skins, and the works had a "rop shop", where they were thoroughly cleaned and produced wholesale to make delicious beef and pork bangers.

The place was heaving with rats, whose staple diet was the firm's bonemeal and animal fat, and, with a stagnant oasis called Owd Nick's Pond close by to slake their thirst, they bred relentlessly.

Those long hot summer days were unforgettable. Apart from the stench from their produce, thousands of flies swarmed the streets — indoors and out. Those yellow twisted fly-catchers hung from living-room ceilings were soon smothered with the dead and dying and had to be changed at regular intervals.

Aye, in the heat of those memorable days, those houses were hot . . . very hot! There were no electric fans in those days. Not down our way, anyroad. No, our ventilation system was simple. Open the front door, open the back door, and close the curtains to keep the sun out.

To open a window could be a little dodgy. They were sash windows and could sometimes be a bugger to open and close, especially if the weighted sash cords had broken. And apart from that problem, a certain amount of dry yellowing rolls of *The Wigan Observer*

24

and *The Wigan Examiner* had to be removed, because that was part of our winter's heating system.

Every year, when winter arrived, and they were gradely winters too, those icy winds howling down from the canal bank and past the boneworks would whistle through those generous window gaps, up skirts and trouser legs, threatening to amputate certain parts of one's anatomy. Those gaps were that wide, you could pop your hand through and wave to a passing neighbour. And that's the truth . . . Well, nearly.

Pegging a rug was one sure way of avoiding this painful experience, because, as every working-class Wiganer will tell you, sitting in front of the fireplace draping a length of hessian sacking over your knees whilst pegging bits of coloured cloth into it was a certain way of keeping the blood flowing.

There was one thing for sure, though — repairs of any kind, whether it was painting, papering or plastering, were never done by the landlord. Accidentally broken windows had to be replaced by the tenant or puttied along the crack to hold it together.

Over the winter months, oil lamps, even candles in bottles and jars, were placed close to the outside lavatory water pipes to prevent a burst or freeze-up. If you were unlucky enough to have a leak — and with the landlord working on the assumption that a burst would only occur again — he left well alone, and you had to carry water from the house to the lavvy till spring arrived.

They still called for the weekly rent though. Miss Ballard, our landlady, did her own collecting and would always quote to Mam, at regular intervals, the following: "Halfpennies make pennies, pennies make shillings and shillings make pounds." Then the cheeky sod would pocket our money and initial the rent book before skipping off to another des res (or should I say, another *un*desirable residence) round the corner.

Believe it or not, until Dad fashioned a crude coal bunker in the yard, our coal was kept under our uncarpeted stairs near the backdoor.

When coal was in short supply, which was often, Dad and I would push Grandad's wheelbarrow to the gasworks (Sovreign Road end), fill a couple of sacks with coke (a shilling a bag, if I remember rightly) and trundle them home.

Now coke was a devil to stoke and keep burning, so you needed a few pieces of wood, a few bits of coal (if you were lucky to have any), a shovel and a sheet of *The Wigan Observer* placed against the fireplace, and away it went; but it still required plenty of attention.

However, not everyone resorted to this way of keeping the home fires burning. Adjacent to Miry Lane, and by the side of nearby railway sidings, tons of coal were piled high into miniature mountains awaiting collection and transportation to other areas. And, as Oscar Wilde once said, "The only way to beat temptation is to give in to it." And quite a few desperate locals did just that. Prams, bikes, trucks and barrows (and, of course, strong shoulders) were brought into play to ferry that precious fuel from track to grate. But this was a somewhat risky business. Railway police and the bobby on the beat had to be avoided, and one chap had a unique, almost infallible method of eluding capture.

Occasionally, he would borrow — yes, borrow — a neighbour's pram and baby — yes, the baby too — and he would meander down to the sidings. On arriving, the infant was placed carefully on a nice patch of grass while he surreptitiously filled a sack with coal, placed it in the pram, covered it well with blankets and sat the baby gently on top. The return journey, although somewhat slower and arduous, was usually made with the child sleeping blissfully on a pile of ill-gotten (but necessary) gains.

How on earth did we ever manage in those years of austerity? No TVs, toasters, telephones, Hoovers, central heating or double-glazing. No carpeted bedrooms or stairs, no electric lights. A stone-flagged living room with a solid square dining table in the middle and one gas mantle above it (and God help anyone who broke a precious mantle).

"DO YOU REMEMBER?"

The list and the memories go on and on. However, there was one luxury (apart from our black-leaded fire range, of course) and that was our acid-battery wireless in the corner. A miracle of modern invention.

And towering above all our adversities was Dad — unflappable, strong, reliable — and Mam cooking, cleaning, scrubbing, washing, darning and knitting. She ran our house with love, discipline and tact, which largely went unnoticed and unappreciated. Deep in the cobwebs of my mind, I can still hear her voice echoing up our rickety stairs and into the bedroom.

"Edward! Edward! Are you out of bed, yet? C'mon, you're goin' to be late for school."

I didn't want to go to school, but I knew if I lingered much longer, it would mean a cold wet flannel across my face.

And that was how it used to be. Dire circumstances, hard work, discipline and Mam's loving, caring hand that fashioned and shaped our very lives and changed the very meaning of the term property from "A Two Up-Two Down Terraced House, Landlord Owned" to: "OUR HOUSE".

"DO YOU REMEMBER?"

CHAPTER
THREE

Life's a Gamble

Foreword
The story that follows isn't about any one particular
character, but is an amalgam of many characters that I
had the honour to have known.

In those distant days of dire circumstances, many of
my neighbours, in a vain attempt to improve their lot in
life, became addicted to gambling in all its various
forms.

This is their story.

Some men, women too, just love to gamble. The thrill
of "having a go" becomes an obsession, and, like some
evil drug, takes control of their lives.

Even before the advent of bingo, lotto, scratch
card and the lottery, there was always numerous
ways of placing a bet, to take a chance of making
some extra money. Besides, to have a little extra cash
is comforting; it makes living a little easier, less of a
trouble and strain. Something extra in the back
pocket or purse does you good; your jaundiced
outlook on life becomes less jaundiced and a little
more optimistic.

And that is why working-class people love to take a risk. A silver lining in a humdrum life of poverty is good for the soul.

Back then, in The Depression, when a game of chance was limited to "doing the pools", backing horses and dogs, playing cards, pitch-and-toss, dominoes and even darts, it was still the excitement of the unknown and the slim chance that a particular gamble would pay off that drove them on. Near misses didn't deter their enthusiasm to try again and again and again.

Many "systems" that guaranteed success were invented. Lucky charms, the name of a certain racehorse or greyhound that was synonymous with a family name or a certain occurrence that had befallen that eager punter, were pounced upon, noted, underlined and used as a regular method that would give them the win of a lifetime. Even Jack Dash, the bookie's runner, who knew all there was to know about the precarious gaming world of racehorses and greyhounds, struggled to take advantage of his boss, the wealthy bookmaker.

Inevitably, some punters became disenchanted with these gambling ventures and turned to the more nefarious pastime of robbing. Not post offices, shops or frail old ladies — those times and wicked ways were still in the distant future. No, the disillusioned residents of Mayflower Road and their nearby neighbours, raided adjacent railway sidings for coal and foraged for wood, any kind and anybody's wood, that could be used as kindling to fire that same coal in empty fire grates and give these suppliers a few extra shillings to spend as they wished.

For others, this pursuit of false happiness convinced them that "luck" could be bought in the shape of lucky charms like Cornish Pixies, four-leafed clover and bracelets, and they would visit fortune tellers, palm readers and those turbaned ladies who read tea leaves.

Then, of course, there were those who just didn't give a damn and spent what little money they had on modest pleasures, even though this meant getting drunk quite often and puffing away happily on their favourite fags.

But even this type of person, devoid of any get-rich-quick notions, sometimes (but very seldom) became an innocent victim of our ever-vigilant police force.

Every week, the brothers John and Harry Bradwell had a Sunday lunchtime booze-up at the Three Crowns pub in Mayflower Road. John was married and lived the other side of town but never failed to meet up with his young, bachelor brother, Harry, for those very enjoyable sessions. A few pints till closing time, then down the road to their mother's for a generous helping of Lancashire hotpot and red cabbage.

This particular Sunday, however, Mrs Bradwell, who was just recovering from a bout of influenza, was running late.

"C'mon, kid," John said. "Let's take a walk till it's ready."

That late September Sunday was warm and sunny, so a stroll by the canal was just the thing to sharpen the appetite. After crossing Elston Bridge, they left the towpath and took a narrow, grassy track that meandered past a disused sewerage works and onwards to an equally disused clay pit. Seated in a tight circle close to the clay pit, a group of men were playing cards. The very remoteness of this card school gave every indication that the stakes were high — very high.

"That's odd," John said.

"What's odd?" Harry said.

"No lookout, they've posted no lookout."

"I can't imagine they'll be needing one out here; I mean, it's not as though they're on a street corner, is it?"

As if in defiance of Harry's flippant remark, from the tall grass and uneven terrain, sprang several uniformed and plain-clothes policemen; with an urgent shout of warning from one of the gamblers, the card school scattered in all directions, each intent on making his escape.

"C'mon, kid," John shouted. "Run for it."

"Bugger off, we're not wi' that lot."

"The bloody cops'll think differently, you idiot; run!"

And with a panting plain-clothes policeman just yards behind, the brothers set off at a gallop.

Ahead lay a busy main road; if they could make it to there, their chances of escape would be greatly improved.

A belly full of beer and some urgent running didn't mix very well, and the two men were fast becoming exhausted, but on reaching the welcoming firmness of the street pavement, they renewed their efforts. The policeman, still only yards behind, began to shout; the brothers ran faster. In the distance a double-decker bus was just taking on a couple of passengers.

"Quick!" panted John. "On that bus . . . quick!"

The bus began to move off. An extra last gasping spurt, and a leap onto the platform, left a frustrated, red-faced copper, cursing in their wake. On arriving home, the reticent duo ate a hearty meal that only honest, true innocents of this uncertain world, can really appreciate.

Now Jack Dash, the bookie's runner, was a no-nonsense bloke, who liked a flutter as much as his "customers" did. But Jack only placed his bets on a horse or greyhound that boasted good form, such as a sure favourite or a consistent runner-up. But he never did hit that desirable jackpot. There was only ever going to be one winner: the bookmaker.

But Jack just loved to gamble. Apart from horses and dogs, Jack would take a gamble on, or with, anything: cards, pitch-and-toss, football pools, anything. And it was these precarious gambles that gave Jack his speed and craftiness.

There was not one single Wigan cop who could outrun him. Many had tried. A lookout's warning cry of, "The cops!" had many a frequent gambling school running like the clappers for the sanctuary of a neighbour's house or some other place of concealment, but no one could overtake Jack Dash. With the speed of a whippet, he was always in the lead: a dash through a house, a vault over a yard wall, a dive into the canal. It was all the same to Jack; he was an escape artist, but has he often wryly commented, "The only person ever to collar me was that bloody wife o' mine, and I ended-up gettin' a bloody life sentence."

Paul and Connie Cotton were the most recently married couple in Mayflower Road. Connie was pregnant and had given up her job at Blakes Cotton Mill to prepare for the coming event of motherhood.

And Paul, well Paul was fortunate; he was employed as a labourer by the local corporation water department. Although digging holes and trenches was very hard going, the work was never rushed. However, because he was new to the job, the chances of any overtime went to the longer-serving and more experienced employees, which left Paul frustrated and desperate.

A rented house, a pregnant wife, a new Singer sewing machine and furniture still to be paid for made life a constant struggle. And his mother-in-law didn't help matters, when, on many occasions, she would indicate to Connie's swollen stomach and say, in her down-to-earth manner, "That's only a start, my girl; you don't open t'oven door for one bun."

Even so, Paul was too proud to go begging, cap in hand for overtime. That wasn't his way. His strength lay in his pride.

He did, however, as do all of us, have his weaknesses. Paul was greatly influenced by superstition, myth and coincidence and all things associated with good luck and bad luck. To spill salt, to break a mirror, to walk under a ladder, to have a black cat cross one's path, were all taboo. And then there were those dark, ominous dreams.

His mother-in-law had once won a goldfish at a visiting fair, and in a gesture of unusual kindness, had bought a goldfish bowl and gave her prize to her daughter. One night, Paul dreamt the fish had died. On remembering the dream the following morning, Paul went straight to the bowl, and sure enough, the fish was a floating, scaly corpse, which, of course, reinforced his belief in dreams, coincidence and the rest.

And this became part of Paul's psychic belief that good fortune, too, could be harnessed, studied and put to good use.

Now, in these bygone times of want, even with the scarcity of money, every Friday a husband always handed over his unopened wage packet, and his wife, depending on the amount received, handed back a shilling or two for him to spend as he pleased, which was usually on beer and fags or the odd flutter. Obviously, poor wages meant less pocket money, and this was Paul Cotton's dilemma. With a baby on the way, and money owed for their domestic appliances and furniture, should he hand over the lot and lose his man-of-the-house status? Or take his well-earned share and use it to try and improve their lot in life? Convinced that his and his pregnant wife's destiny was his sole responsibility, and his alone, he took the money.

He then began to speculate. Unlike Jack Dash, who would invent "systems" and study the form of horses and dogs, Paul used what he thought were his psychic powers. Forever vigilant to the names of people, occurrences and incidents that were closely linked to the names of racehorses and greyhounds, he would, without hesitation, place his bets.

Paul, for all his wayward methods of speculation, was sensitive to the fact that if he used the services of Jack Dash and Jack's boss, he would be ridiculed, and if not confronted with ridicule, Paul knew that local punters would soon become aware of his methods, and that would never do; if word got back to Connie of his new addiction, there would be serious trouble, especially if Connie's mother found out as well. Paul shuddered at the thought.

So Paul, with a craftiness that comes with the law of self-preservation, began to frequent a betting shop in the town centre. But his devious perseverance proved fruitless. As his futile attempts to make money became more and more desperate, Paul became more and more irritable and confused.

One Saturday afternoon, with a few shillings in his pocket, Paul headed once again for town. On this day, he decided to take a short cut through Wigan Park. His mind was in turmoil, but his eyes missed nothing. If only there was some sort of sign, some kind of symbol for him to find some inspiration before reaching the betting shop.

But as he walked on, his determination to succeed began to diminish. It was hopeless.

★　★　★

And in a fog of despair, Paul, feeling utterly wretched and worthless, barely noticed him. Then the mist of misery cleared.

SIR FRANCIS SHARP POWELL, BARONET.
BORN IN WIGAN 1827. MP FOR HIS NATIVE
TOWN 1857–9 AND 1885–1910 ERECTED BY
PUBLIC SUBSCRIPTION 1910.

Paul stopped and couldn't take his eyes off him.

He'd been sat there since 1910 in his big, comfortable chair, chin resting on the thumb of his right hand, with legs casually crossed and one foot forward, inviting all and sundry to give his already shiny shoe a rub for good luck. Because that's what some Wigan folk, who believed in this long-standing ritual did. They gave that shiny shoe a good rub for luck.

Paul looked about. The park was almost empty, just an old lady with shopping bags, a mother and child, and a tramp sitting on a nearby bench.

Feeling somewhat embarrassed, Paul stepped forward, stood on the plinth, reached up and gave the shoe a vigorous rub. At least he was trying his best. He couldn't wait to get to that betting shop. He hurried on.

He was well spoken, definitely not a local man. Could be from the southern regions. Paul was undecided.

"Excuse me, sir."

Paul stopped. He thought the tramp was about to ask for money. His overcoat was shabby, and he was in need of a shave. At his feet was a small, battered suitcase.

"Am I to assume that that there statue is some kind of talisman?"

"If you mean does rubbing his shoe bring luck, I don't know for sure."

"Then why in God's name do it?"

"Because everyone else seems to do it."

"So there's no concrete evidence that this practice of polishing the shoe of a long-dead baronet brings any gain whatsoever."

"How did you know he was a baronet?"

"Because I'm a very inquisitive person. I've been using this lovely park for quite a while now and have seen men, women and children doing what you've just done . . . Well, I couldn't resist taking a peep to see who the gentleman was."

"You're not from these parts are you?"

"No. Let's say I'm a travelling optimist."

"A what?"

"I move along in the hope that somewhere, at sometime or other, my journey will come to an end in a most pleasant manner."

"Have you no family?"

He laughed. "I left them behind to seek my fortune and a better life."

"Then I think you'd better do some foot rubbing yourself," Paul said.

"I'm happy enough doing what I'm doing. I don't believe in myth nor magic; life's a gamble and you take your chances."

"So by abandoning your family and friends for this better life, as you call it, you also left behind your worries and responsibilities . . . that's not a gamble, that's cowardly."

"Maybe so, but sometimes cowardice is the only means of escape."

Paul shook the stranger's hand. "Who am I to judge anyone? You're doing what you have to do, and that's the end of it. I'm off now to do what I've got to do. Goodbye, whoever you are."

The tramp smiled. "And good luck."

As he was leaving the park, Paul thought back to breakfast time. He was almost sure he'd read something about a tramp in the morning paper. Now that would definitely be a lucky coincidence. Just think. Meeting a tramp and rubbing Mr Powell's foot, all within a matter of minutes.

His heart skipped a beat. He hurried on. He couldn't wait to get to that betting shop.

"Do You Remember?"
That Mon in t' Park

"DO YOU REMEMBER?"

"I'm cowder than that mon in t' park."

Can you remember when you last heard that familiar, old Wigan saying? (Meaning, of course, the seated figure of Sir Francis Sharp Powell, MP and Baronet)

I say it on a regular basis, because I'm one of those unfortunate characters with "thin blood". I'm always "cowd": hands, feet, face and body, the lot! But I don't moan about it . . . Well, not much. But I'll tell you what, this last winter 2009–10 (the coldest for 3 decades, or so they tell us) really tested me, and I must admit, I did my share of complaining.

But what a carry on with the media. TV, radio and newspapers latched on to those atrocious conditions like it had never happened before. The weather had more coverage than World War Two. What with those never-ending, dismal, gloomy weather reports coming at us from all sides and the recession, I felt like topping myself. Why carry on? I thought. Freezing to death and no jingle in mi pocket to cheer me up. Where will it all end?

Then I began to remember. I began to think back about the winters of times gone by. And every winter was the same. Feet-deep snowfalls that temporarily changed the character of our towns, cities and countryside, not flakes of snow floating down to earth like moon dust. And frost that held with an iron-like grip for weeks on end, fracturing pipes and transforming our miserable houses into bricks and mortar fridges with one coal fire struggling in vain to keep us warm.

"DO YOU REMEMBER?"

As an employee of the newly-formed Makerfield Water Board, I remember especially the winter of 1962–63. It was certainly the most damaging I've ever experienced, and it lasted for 3 long months without a let-up. The cold was so severe that frost went into the ground to a depth of 2 feet or more and consequently was responsible for countless burst mains and services, which left in their wake collapsed roads and flooded houses. No sooner had one burst main been repaired, than it burst again further along the road. Twelve burst mains in one day occurred in Hindley alone. We worked day and night to keep supplies going and the waste of water to a minimum.

When I visited one old lady at her home on Worsley Hall Estate, her ceiling had collapsed because of a burst water tank. One week later, I made a return visit to

42

discover she'd had another burst and yet more damage to her home, but her only comment was, "It's a reet bad winter we're havin', int it, lad?" No hysterics. No self-pity. Just a simple statement from a sturdy old lady who showed a strength of character that is sadly lacking in today's namby-pamby world of groaners and moaners.

Aye, it was a bad un, and we, like everyone else, skidded, cursed and shivered our way through, and never thought once about giving up the struggle. And we even had our moments of joy and amazement.

One day, a colleague and I received a radio call to investigate a suspected burst main not far from the village of Parbold. It was a burst all right. The main, which ran through some woodland had fractured, sending a fountain of water high into the air and showering the surrounding trees and bushes. The scene was unbelievable. In the intense cold, the water had immediately frozen, and there, in front of us, stood several of nature's very own decorative, tinkling, shimmering Christmas trees — a spectacular winter wonderland and one which I shall always remember.

Nevertheless, although my working days are long gone, I don't want to experience another winter like 1962–63. So, to be on the safe side, I've been doing some deep thinking. Early on, before winter sets in, I'm going to visit that mon in t' park. I can see him now, chin resting on the thumb of his right hand and that steady, thoughtful gaze looking down at me. Then I'm going to give that shiny shoe of his a vigorous rub and make a wish, and that wish will be for a mild winter;

because, you see, I don't want to steal the man's reputation. I don't want to be cowder than him. I don't want folk passing me in t' street and nudging one another and saying, "Look at him . . . He looks cowder than that mon in t' park."

Anyroad, who knows what the future will bring. I mean, what will happen when full-scale global warming arrives? Will his reputation go up in smoke? (so to speak). Personally, I don't think so. I think us Wigan folk will always be shivering and blowing on our digits in the middle of winter and cursing like hell and saying, "I'm cowder than that mon in t' park."

CHAPTER
FOUR

Catch-as-Catch-Can

A stranger once asked of Mayflower Road, "Where does this road lead to?" And was told, quite positively, "Follow your nose till tha comes to the boneworks, then with the stench behind you, tha'll be on t' canal bank, and that's about it."

And those directions almost sum up the place where I was born and raised. Was it really a road going nowhere? Well, for starters, our part of Mayflower Road was somewhat isolated from the rest. We lived at the tail end, hemmed in by a low, main-line railway bridge, a canal and a confusion of railway sidings and locomotive repair sheds. The place was incredibly unique, and with no houses opposite, our little palace was the last one in Mayflower Road.

Once past us, there was a stretch of uneven, ungrassed land that we called the back field; it took you to the very perimeter of our salubrious boneworks, which was just a spit away from the canal. But before stepping onto this untended adopted play area, turn sharp right, and you were in Hurrydown Lane. No one knew why a dead-end street had been given the grand title of Lane, but there you have it. Mayflower Road,

Hurrydown Lane, a setting that housed a collection of unforgettable characters, who lived in unforgettable times.

A few of my best mates lived in Hurrydown Lane: Kenny "Picky" Coleman, who was forever picking his nose; "Birdy" Briggs who only ever stopped whistling to eat and talk (and I don't know whether she was kidding me are not, but his mam always said he even whistled in his sleep). But best of them all was Richie Fenton. We got on well, did Richie and me. Richie was our gang leader, and his daring and ingenuity were exemplary. He was afraid of nothing nor no one was Richie.

With money in short supply, everyone was on the lookout to acquire some. Whoever coined the phrase, "What you don't have, you can manage without" or "What you've never had, you don't miss" must have been an idiot, because for us and everyone else in our community, money was for our every day existence: food, warmth, clothing and that all-important rent. We had none to squander, that's for sure.

For us, banks didn't exist. No one put money into a bank; (ironically) they couldn't afford it. Saving a little for essentials, like a Sunday roast, birthday and Christmas presents, was an accepted procedure, and that was it.

Anyway, I digress. Richie Fenton was a genious with fantastic ideas. Now the landlord of the Three Crowns public house on Mayflower Road put all of his empty beer and pop bottles back in crates and stacked them in his pub yard to await the draymen's delivery and collection day, and Richie, who happened to be passing the pub on one of these days, hit on the idea of "Bottle Snatching". A raid was planned.

One Saturday night, when the alehouse was busy, we hopped over the yard wall, gathered a few pop bottles from the bottom crates and, over the next few days, handed them back to an unsuspecting landlord for money on the returns, which, although only coppers, bought us Wild Woodbine fags and toffee from Mrs Ashurst's little shop.

Not far from Mayflower Road there was a rag-and-bone yard where all the local rag-and-bone men sold their daily collections. Richie tried to muscle in on this once lucrative business. Under his instructions, we began our own collections: bicycle parts, old clothing, jam jars, copper, iron — anything and everything that was collectable was gathered by any means possible (fair or foul) and taken by barrow, bike and bag to the yard, and we were well rewarded for our efforts. We called these one-off occasions, "Collection Days". "Bottle Snatching" and "Collection Days". That's why Richie was our gang leader. He was bold, confident and inventive, and we could always rely on him for leadership and a little extra pocket money.

The house where Richie lived was quite unusual for our run-down area; it boasted a front parlour, and sometimes, especially on Saturday nights when Richie's parents had gone out for a few beers, and his sister, Sally, was out playing street games, the gang would use the parlour for a variety of activities. It also became . . . well, a sort of "classroom" where certain games were played, confidences exchanged and confusing information of a sexual nature given free rein.

Sometimes, but only with Richie's permission, girls were invited to join the group, and a game of "Spin the Bottle" was the highlight of the evening. An empty bottle was placed in the centre of the kneeling circle (arranged boy, girl, boy, girl) and spun around; when the bottle stopped spinning, whoever the neck of the bottle was pointing to had to remove an article of clothing, and, with a boyish sleight of hand, the neck always, without fail, pointed excitingly to one of the girls. Soon, the lot of them were down to their knickers and vests, while we males, now excited to the point of bursting, tried our very best to take matters to a heartbeat-skipping full strip. But those young temptresses, knowing the minds and nature of our devious schemes, became giggly, coy, non-cooperative and less provocative.

Somehow or other (perhaps because her brother was always present), Sally Fenton never took part in these risqué games, but that didn't make me less lustful. Her full bosom, long auburn hair and bluest of blue eyes set in a heart-wrenchingly pretty face made my secret desire for her almost unbearable. And the bottling up of this passion had an awfully embarrassing effect. Every time we met, I blushed the colour of crimson.

Then, tragedy struck. Sally caught some kind of mystery virus that affected her brain. Within weeks, she was dead.

This catastrophe was apparent in the neighbourhood. From that awful moment on, everyone seemed to be in shock. They even talked in hushed tones as this unbelievable disaster took hold. I, too, was overcome by grief, misery and self-pity.

Gertrude Slonker, Mrs. Fenton's cousin, and Mrs Green, a neighbour, went from house to house collecting money for a neighbourhood wreath, which was then placed on a dining chair under Mrs Fenton's front window, a gesture that gave everyone the chance to see what their few pennies had been spent on. Later in the day, it was moved indoors close to the coffin, which rested on two wooden trestles in the very same parlour where our amorous games had been played.

The day of the funeral was the saddest day of my life. The streets were lined with tearful, sobbing friends and neighbours. I think everyone was crying — except for one person. Richie. Richie was strangely dry-eyed. Pale, shrunken and distant, yes, but showing no grief whatsoever. And what was about to follow seemed to me, at the time, as sorrowful, tragic and as emotional as Sally's death.

Two days after the funeral, I went round to Richie's house. Mrs Fenton answered my knock.

"Is Richie in?"

"He's in but that's about all."

"Is he coming out?"

"Now there's a problem."

I didn't understand these evasive replies. "Is he ill, Mrs Fenton?"

"He's not been the same since our Sally's death . . . he's not eating properly, he won't talk, he doesn't want to go out, and he's awake half the night with bad dreams . . . I can hear him shouting and muttering."

"What kind of dreams?"

"He won't say, and all this has happened since our poor Sally left us."

"He'll come round," I said. "He's still upset. He's still in shock, you know, and who can blame him. I'll call round next week."

But the following week was just the same. Time and time again I called on him, but he wouldn't even come to the door. Even school was ruled out. His parents were desperately worried. Richie refused to see Doctor Merry, so his mother asked the good doctor to call and see him, and he just reiterated what everyone else already knew. Richie's depression was due to his sister's untimely death. There was no medicinal cure. There was only one person with the answer to Richie's mental sickness — Richie himself, and if it didn't happen soon, the boy could even lose the will to live.

But doctors don't know it all. And sometimes even the most humble of our society can step into the shoes of the educated and academic classes with unbelievable aptitude and that infinite quality that is the mainstay of the lower-classes. Common sense.

Gertrude Slonker was big and blunt and a spinster, and she was Richie Fenton's aunt and lived three doors away in Hurrydown Lane. The house, humble, but clean, with sparkling windows and lace curtains, boasted one framed photograph only: a black and white one of a stocky, burly, unsmiling man in trunks, who by the looks of his menacing pose was about to give the photographer a life-threatening bear hug. This was George Slonker, Gertrude's brother, who, apart from working in an iron foundry, was an amateur wrestler and grappled under the name of "Iron Man" Slonker. He was the first of our neighbours to go to war and the first to get killed.

Just like her brother, Gertrude, too, went into action. Not in uniform, no gun, just with plain common sense.

Now, Jeremiah Johnson (his name was too much of a mouthful for us, so we called him JJ) was supposed be suffering from some kind of heart problem, but every year, when it was harvest time for those essential staple vegetables, potatoes and peas, off he went by rail to distant farmlands to do some spud and pea picking. Someone once said he had even travelled down south for the hop-picking season.

Anyway, Gertrude persuaded JJ to take Richie with him on those harvesting excursions, and oddly enough, Richie complied. But Gertrude's "curative" plan didn't have the results she had hoped for. Although working in the fields at the height of good weather gave Richie a burnished, healthy glow and made him seem physically stronger, psychologically, he was unchanged; still reticent, still morose and moody, and, once back home from his labouring, stayed indoors.

Every Monday morning, Gertrude Slonker walked into town to do a little shopping, and, on her way home, she always called at Bert Wilson's tripe shop; three penn'orth of tripe bits, smothered in salt, pepper and vinegar, washed down with a glass of milk stout she had purchased from the pub next door, and she was a happy woman.

Now I remember this particular Monday very well indeed, because that morning, Gertrude had done a little extra shopping, and it was smack in the middle of our summer holidays, and I received this baffling request to call on her.

"Now, lad," she said. "I've heard talk that you're our Richie's best mate . . . is that right?"

"We're like brothers, Mrs Slonker."

"Don't call me missus, lad, I'm not married, so I'm not a missus."

I was stumped. "Then what do I call you, missus . . . er . . ."

"Just call me Gertrude or Gert, any one will do. So, you're like brothers, eh?"

"I'll do anything for Richie, anything."

"You know what ails him, don't you?"

"Doctor Merry says . . ."

"Aye, an' I know that Doctor Merry's given up on him, and he expects to sit on his backside and hope for a miracle."

"He will get better, won't he?"

"You'll get him better, lad."

"Me?" I burst out laughing. "How the 'eck can I do owt for Richie?"

Without another word, Gertrude went through to her back kitchen and reappeared holding a book. "While I was out shopping, I bought this. Go on have a look, because the contents of that book are going to cure our Richie, and you're going to help him."

I read the title: *Catch-As-Catch-Can*, and in the centre of its shiny cover, a half-naked, moderately built man with cauliflower ears was posing in an aggressive grappling stance. And below the photograph, in bold letters, were the words: "The author, Captain S. G. Strong, England's unbeaten, middleweight champion, confidently assures that his style of wrestling will make anyone, if not a world champion, then a confident exponent of this form of self-defence."

The book was packed throughout with fine-line drawings of various wrestling holds and throws and each with appropiate, detailed instructions.

"But how is this going to help Richie?" I said.

"Because our Richie needs some physical contact, that's why. He needs to let go. He must become forceful and self-assertive, and that must come by taking his bottled-up frustrations out on something or someone"

"And that someone is me, is it? In other words you want him to half-kill me in the process."

"I only wish our George were still with us," Gertrude said

"So do I," I said.

"You're our only chance, Eric, but you'll have to approach him careful, like; you know, use a bit o' tact. And remember, don't let on that it were my idea. He might take offence."

For the next couple of days, I did quite a bit of pondering on Gertrude's wily scheme; then out of the blue, it came to me. I wrote Richie a note, and before popping it through the letterbox, read it aloud:

"Hi, Richie,

it's me, your owd mate, Eric. Since you've been off school, I've been picked on by Jack Carver, him out of standard 6, so I've bought a book on self-defence, but I need a mate to practise with. Can you help an owd mate, so that I can knock the stuffing out of him. I hope so.

Eric."

A loud knocking on our front door the next day brought me face to face with an unsmiling Richie.

"What's all this crap about self-defence, Eric?"

"Well, it's a book on wrestling really, and I can't wrestle me bloody self, can I? I need a partner."

"Surely tha can beat Jack Carver. He's a bloody puddin'."

"He's bigger than me, though."

"He's still a puddin'. I remember once our Sally givin' him a bloody good thumpin', and if she could do it any bugger can."

I felt an inward surge of hope. If he was talking about and remembering Sally, the breakthrough might be easier than we thought.

"Maybe, but to know a few holds and throws would definitely give me a head start, won't it?"

"C'mon, then, let's have a look at this bloody book o' thine."

"I'll get it an' we'll go down to Gambler's Field, eh?"

Gambler's Field was lush with deep green summer's grass, and the two of us, with the book between us, began to study the contents. A while later, stripped to

54

the waist, we began our first tentative lesson of catch-as-catch-can.

Although our initial efforts were clumsy and obviously very amateurish, I let Richie take the more active part, which included trips, holds and poorly executed throws. A while later, bruised, exhausted and yet exhilarated, we called a halt to this, the first of many lessons.

Gradually, with patience and practice, Gertrude Slonker's shrewd thinking produced results, and Richie became, well, the Richie we all knew: witty, extrovert, confident, and raring to take command of his gang once again.

It was after one particularly strenuous session that I suddenly realised that these catch-as-catch-can lessons would soon come to an end . . . or would they? It was Richie himself who had me thinking otherwise.

"Listen, Eric," he said one day. "I've been doin' some serious thinkin' lately."

"Oh, aye," I said, knowing full well that his serious thinking usually meant concocting one of his daring plans for himself, me, Birdy, Picky and the rest. Things were definitely looking up.

"This wrestling game — it's beginning to get better and better; I like it . . . I think it's in my blood. My uncle George was a wrestler, you know. I just might follow in his footsteps."

Richie Fenton was definitely back with us. I could sense his strength and determination. His voice was urgent and had a passionate, confident ring to it. Yes, Richie was back with a vengeance.

"But you must promise me one thing, Eric."

"Anything, mate, anything."

"Don't let on to Auntie Gertrude about any o' this. It's better if she doesn't know what we've been doing all right? . . . Anyroad, I'd never hear the last of how good a wrestler Uncle George was; she'd give me a load of earache, that's for sure."

"My lips are sealed, mate," I said.

Later that same day, an amusing thought made me smile; Gertrude Slonker and Richie Fenton had just one thing in common: CATCH-AS-CATCH-CAN, and they were both humble champions.

John '10'

"Do You Remember?"
Humble Days, Humble Ways

"DO YOU REMEMBER?"

The longer I live surrounded, confused, bewildered and bedevilled by today's relentless march of technology, the more I seem to retreat into the past. I keep recalling the simplicity of life as it used to be, and which has been obliterated forever. The relentless march of progress has robbed us of certain old-fashioned values and a perseverance that was engraved in the very hearts and minds of our once close-knit communities.

Am I right in thinking that the advance of technology has actually distanced us? We may have televisions, telephones, mobile phones, CDs, MP3 players, computers and cassette players, that, with just a touch of a button, can bring into focus, and within hearing, people who live miles away, the other side of the world even. But this same technology has come between us. It's all too easy (if you know what you're doing!). These tools of technology have taken away the very essence of caring, personal contact, and left us struggling with messages on machines.

And what comes with all this technical stuff? The literature, of course. How to set up, how to assemble and how to fault-find, and best of all, HELPLINE. If you get into trouble, call HELPLINE. Have you ever tried calling HELPLINE for anything? You can get hold of the Pope quicker.

When I was a lad, our clever stuff was in a corner of the living room in Miry Lane, and it was called a wireless. And that was it. The only local phone (apart from a phone box on Wallgate) belonged to the Hollis family, who ran a small haulage business from their home in Prescott Street. There was many a dash to that house in emergencies, like canal drownings or someone taken seriously ill. You still had to cough up a few coppers for the call though.

If someone died a few streets away, ten minutes later the whole neighbourhood knew about it, and what they had died from too. And those same neighbours lined the streets to see him or her carted off to the cemetery three days later.

Now there was one family who, to us anyroad, did own what might be classed as a bit of technology. Well, sort of.

The Clark family lived in Prescott Street (Miry Lane end) and had in a corner of their living room, believe it or not, a massive organ. Not electric, but the pedal type. God only knows where they got it from. But Mrs Clark would often entertain many a passer-by, belting out those popular tunes of the day: *When Poppies Bloom Again; It's Only a Shanty in Old Shanty Town* . . . and so on. When they decided to get shot, it wouldn't go through the door, and it took two days to dismantle it.

And talking about organs, my brother, John, gave vent to his musical talents on a mouth organ, which he played with passion and gusto at every opportunity. He is still fondly remembered for his playing on bonfire nights, which in those days was a more neighbourly get-together occasion.

Every year, we built the biggest and best (as high as Everest) bonfire ont' "back field" at the bottom of Miry Lane. Wood, mattresses, tyres and trees (including a few railway sleepers "donated" by kind-hearted railway workers from nearby sidings) were collected by the Clark brothers, P, Tom and Bill, Henry "Fat" Jennings (although he was never fat), my brothers Tom and John, Jimmy Ainscough and a few others, besides.

Then, with our few fireworks spent, spuds roasting in the embers and Mam's home-made treacle toffee doing the rounds, the singing to our John's harmonica playing began. And one song went like this:

Way down in Texas, back in my home town,
   A gang of rustling cowboys shot my old man down.
   Now the man who did this killing, they called him Trigger Kid,
   And I swore that I would get him if it was the last thing I did.
   So I joined the Texas Rangers to see what I could do.
   The Captain said,. "The life is tough, but we're needin' men like you."

60

There was me and Pete and Lefty, we tracked those outlaws down,

We found them in a barroom in a outlaw border town.

They shot up Pete and Lefty as they were on the run.

So I pulled out my 45er and I shot them one by one.

By 'eck! Now that's what I call a proper neighbourly do; sitting round a bonfire scoffing home-made stuff and singing our bloody heads off to a humble mouth organ. Unforgettable!

"DO YOU REMEMBER?"

CHAPTER
FIVE

"A New Beginning, Begins"

The living room was a motley mix of old and new furniture, and seated side by side on a new settee, Frances and Tom, each holding a mug of tea, sat silent, each in their own way, thinking back on what had been and what was to come.

"This is it, Tom," Frances said. "A new beginning, begins, and I never thought in a million years that it would ever happen."

"Oh, it's happened," Tom said. "And it's been damned hard work too, I'm getting too old for this sort o' thing."

"One thing's for sure," Frances said. "Our next move will be in a wooden box."

"You'll live till you're a hundred, woman."

"I doubt it, but like I said, my next bit o' furniture will be a plain wooden box."

"Don't be a misery, woman. One minute you're talking about a new beginning, and in t' next breath you're talking about clocking off."

Tom looked up at the low ceiling and the four paperless, magnolia-coloured walls.

"Well, I won't be needing a ladder to decorate this lot."

"There you go again — all you think about is decoratin'."

"You've got to keep your hand in."

"It'll be ages before this lot needs any slap-dash; anyway, there's a garden out back and a new garden gate wanted to keep it private, like."

"Now, now, Frances, don't get stuck-up just because you've moved into a new bungalow."

"Stuck-up, me? Now let's not forget one thing, Tom; it's a council bungalow, not ours."

"Who'd ah thought, Frances — a garden at our age."

"Aye, it's a bit bigger than that window box we had on t' backroom window sill."

"It is an' all."

"This would 'ave killed your dad, Tom."

"You mean, movin' house . . . movin' here?"

"Admit it, that allotment back o' their house kept him goin' after leavin' t' canal."

"So it did. Both o' them, Mam and Dad, spent hours growin' stuff and looking after his hens. It took a while for it to happen though. Dad took it badly. He still had Jenny his faithful mare to contend with; he didn't want to part wi' her."

"This were before we got wed, Tom. What happened, really?"

Tom drained his cup. "Well, you know he used to stable Jenny on t' allotment . . ."

"I know that."

". . . well, when he were forced to finish work, he couldn't afford to keep her in feed, and he didn't want her to go to the knacker's yard."

"Can't blame him for that."

"So he walked her down to the Three Crowns, up the steps and straight into the vault and tried to sell her off."

"Now I ask you," Frances said. "Who on earth would want a flamin' boat horse down our way?"

Tom gave her a withering look. "The man was desperate, woman; he didn't know which way to turn . . . and he were drunk . . . and he once trundled Mam's Singer sewing machine down there an' tried to flog that too . . . he were drunk that time, as well."

"Poor soul!"

"Jenny had to be put-down eventually. It were after that he concentrated more on his allotment; sellin' eggs and lettuce and rhubarb and suchlike."

"I remember that alright," Frances said. "And like I said, this way o' life would have killed him off for sure."

"You're probably right. You see, Frances, my ancestors were water gypsies really — canal people — rough and ready folk who worked hard and played even harder and didn't give a damn."

"Wasn't there one called, Dick Tupp?"

"Richard Darren, that were his proper name; he were mi dad's cousin, an' he were big, strong, a hard drinker, an' a hard man to tangle with, who feared nowt nor nobody."

"Wasn't there something about him breaking a tiled fireplace?"

"Apparently, that's how he got this nickname, 'Dick Tupp'. He'd stopped off at this canal-side pub to do some carousing, and somebody challenged him to smash this fireplace with his fist."

"You mean, give it a thump, like?"

"That's right. But he wouldn't; if he had damaged his hand he wouldn't 'ave been able to do his job o' work, would he?"

"So he used his head instead?"

"That's right. He knelt in front of the fireplace, took off his cloth cap and gave it an almighty headbutt an' shattered the bugger . . . an' from that day on he were always known as Dick Tupp."

"And is it true, Tom?"

"'Course it's true, an' I'll tell you summat for nowt, because of that bloody head of his, not one so-called, battling boatee would square up to him ever again."

"There were some right characters among you lot, I must say."

Tom grinned. "Aye, but we've mellowed with age."

Frances gave him a knowing look. "That's right; you're more for gardening and making garden gates these days."

"And what comes after, woman? What next? There's no decoratin' to be done, an' come winter, there'll be no gardening, either, and if you think I'm goin' to gawp at that tele all day, you can think again."

"You'll think o' summat."

"Such as? We've got central heating, so there's no kindling to chop, no coal to bring in; tell me woman, how do I keep going?"

"You'll think o' summat."

"Stop repeating yoursel', woman."

"Don't get ratty with me. Thomas."

Tom stood up and went to the window, hands deep in pockets.

"I'll do plenty o' walking, that's what I'll do. We're not that far from the canal bank . . . That's it, I'll walk and do some remembering."

"I said you'd think o' summat."

"Have you noticed, Frances, how many faces you see at the windows round here? They're like bloody prisoners. No street corner chats like you used to have . . . if they're not staring at the bloody tele, they're gawping through the bloody window."

"We'll make new friends, Tom, and besides, Betty and Freddy Bell have moved up this way. I'll find out where and we'll call and have a good natter about the old days."

Tom was still at the window. "If I remember rightly, you couldn't stand Betty, bloody, Bell; you hated the sight of her."

"But it's different now, Tom. We're livin' in a different world; we've got to cling on to something or someone from the past. Times have changed."

"Too bloody true."

"Then there's our Albert and Pauline and little David — they'll be visitin'."

"I don't think there'll be many visits from that quarter."

"Why not?"

"Because they'll be splittin' up, that's why."

"I must admit our Bert never mentions Pauline these days, an' we've never seen her for ages."

"Well, there you go then."

"But it shouldn't stop our Bert bringing young David round to see us, surely."

"Don't hold your breath, woman."

"It's like we're livin' on another planet, Tom; nothing's the same."

"It's called progress, Frances; if you get fed up with anything, throw it out the window . . . and that means your marriage vows, too."

"It never used to be like that; marriage was for life. Look at us."

"Aye, a bloody life sentence."

"At least we pulled together and made it work."

"I believe it were the struggle just to keep our heads above water that kept us together, Frances."

"You're probably right. We hadn't the time to dwell nor the money to spend on things we knew we couldn't have; we just got on with livin' best road we could."

Tom sat down. "Thinkin' back, Frances, we always lived within our means. We saved up for what we wanted; you did the cooking and baking — meals made from nowt, and bloody good, too, they were. Clothes patched and repaired . . ."

"And you soled and heeled our shoes, put irons on your work clogs."

"An' you knitted and crocheted and made rugs from sacking and cut-up pieces of clothing."

"There were no plastic cards and money machines in them days, Tom."

"Our bank, for what bit o' money we did have, were that old tea caddy on t' mantlepiece."

"One cold-water tap, and, when we could afford it, a gas geyser so I could wash-up without boilin' t' kettle . . . By the way, Tom, what about this 'ere central heatin'? We'll not know how to work it . . . then there's that newfangled washing machine."

"Aye, a bit more complicated than that dolly tub, rubbing board and bloody mangle we used to have."

"How did we ever manage, Tom, saving pennies for the gas meter and gas mantles . . . and God help anyone who broke one of those."

"Aye, no gaslight meant early to bed or dig out a couple o' candles. All that's behind us now, luv. We've got new neighbours, livin' in new houses and new bungalows, in new roads and avenues, with a whole new way of living."

"But it's the past what makes us what we are. You can't wipe out what we've just been talking about, Tom." Frances snapped her fingers. "Not like that, you can't. You've got to have memories, otherwise we'd be nothing . . . We might as well be dead."

"That's true; that's one thing nobody can take away, your memories. Even if you forget where you've put your soddin' glasses, you always seem to remember what happened donkey's years ago."

"There's one thing I definitely don't remember, Tom."

"And what's that, Frances?"

"I don't remember ever going away on holiday."

"Plenty of our kind never did; it were a struggle just to keep some grub on t' table, though you've got to admit, we did have odd days at Blackpool."

"A day trip on a charabanc wasn't exactly a holiday, Tom."

"You used to enjoy them, didn't you?"

"Course I did, but we've still never had a full week away . . . not even at Blackpool."

"Do folk really need to go on holiday to have a happy married life or to keep the family together? I don't think so, and you can bet there's some of them thinkin' of divorce even while they're jetting off to Spain."

"Do you think we'd better have a telephone installed, Tom?"

"Hell fire, woman, what do we need a phone for?"

"Well, like we said earlier, our Bert's marriage is a bit dodgy and we might have to rely on phone calls to keep in touch."

"He's got a car; he knows where we live. What's to stop him calling round and bringing young David with him?"

"Even so, a phone is always handy, you never know what's going to 'appen at our age. I mean, do you remember that Saturday night when our Bert fell off that old brick air-raid shelter and broke his arm?"

"Like it were yesterday."

"And me walking him up to Wigan Infirmary early Sunday morning?"

"You're probably right about a phone."

"I know I'm right; everyone's got a phone these days. Anyway, now we've gone all posh-like, with a new washer and central heating an' such, we'll need a phone in case any emergencies crop up, like breakdowns and wanting a doctor."

"All right, woman, don't keep chuntering on and on about it. We'll get one fixed, all right?"

"I think your right, you know, Tom."

Tom, with a deep sigh, said, "About what?"

"What you said about holidays and marriage, and that it's the hard times and the struggling what keeps you together."

"Did I say that?"

"Well, that's what you meant . . . I'm like you, money and possessions don't guarantee a happy marriage; they never have."

"It works for some, though. I mean it didn't do Freddy and Betty Bell any harm, did it?"

"How much did they win, Tom?"

"A few hundred."

"Freddy picked 8 draws on t' Littlewoods pools, didn't he?"

"He were a bit unlucky, though. That week there were quite a few drawn games, so there were other winners, otherwise, he'd 'ave definitely hit the jackpot."

Frances sniffed. "It were that win that made Betty what she was."

"Stuck-up, you mean."

"She thought she were lady muck."

"He never changed though; he used to buy rounds o' drinks in t' Three Crowns."

"Uh! Not like her; she started buying new furniture and dressing up like a tart — lipstick an' all."

"They reckon he give quite a sum t' church for the waifs and strays."

"I bet she didn't know about it. She were never the generous type, were Betty; stuck-up bitch."

A knock on their front door interrupted any further condemnations.

"I wonder who that can be? You go, Tom, and see who it is."

The sound of voices filtered through to her. "I'll bet a shilling it's those Jehovah's Witness people." She muttered.

Then Tom's voice, loud, clear and inviting, made her frown with annoyance.

"Good God, the daft sod's invited them in; we'll never get shot."

"You've got visitors, Frances," Tom said.

Frances stood up and turned. She was wrong. Very wrong. It wasn't, as she had expected, two smartly turned-out Jehovah's Witnesses, but Freddy and Betty Bell, faces alight with beaming smiles, arms outstretched invitingly, looking for all the world like two reunited, long-lost friends.

"Betty luv, what a lovely surprise. How on earth did you find us? We've only just this minute been talking about you, haven't we, Tom. Don't just stand there, come in, sit you down. Oh, you've made my day, you have. Tom, don't stand there gawping; have you nothing to say? Take their coats and go and put the kettle on; go on, straighten your face, we've got company."

Tom filled the kettle, brought out the best china, and wondered about the fickleness of the female species, and wondered too about this new beginning on which he and Frances were about to embark.

Even now, surrounded with the luxury of modernity, the past was still with them.

"It's like Frances said," Tom said aloud. "This is where a new beginning, begins; but we and our kind haven't changed one iota. We're still the same, but in a different place, that's all."

John 10

"Do You Remember?"
A Golden Age

"DO YOU REMEMBER?"

Do you remember how many picture houses there were in Wigan's town centre? If, like me, you spent more time visiting these palatial places of entertainment than visiting relatives, you'll remember right enough.

They've all gone now, leaving in their wake an arcade of shops, nightclubs, a car park and swimming baths, but also, thankfully, memories — memories of a golden age of entertainment. Do you remember the Ritz in Station Road? (Even the road has now gone). It was probably the poshest, cleanest and most comfortable one of the lot.

It was at this cinema that I first saw *The Adventures of Robin Hood* with the dashing Errol Flynn as Robin. I think it was 1938, the same year the film was released. Seventy years on, it is still the best Robin Hood film ever.

Just a short walk from the Ritz, tucked away up a narrow passageway (was it called Bretherton's Row?), just off Market Place, was the Empire. I think this was the smallest picture house in town. If you wanted a seat in the "gods" (upstairs), you had to climb an iron fire escape on the side of the building to get there. And I wonder how our present day health and safety brigade would react to that little lot? Probably close the place down, eh?

Another short stroll from where a policeman once carried out his point duties and down Wallgate to the Clarence Hotel was the Princess Cinema, which today goes under the mystical title of Club Nirvana.

I recall once (it must have been about 1941, because the blackout was in force), I and a couple of mates went to see, if I remember right, *The Curse of the Wolfman*, a horror picture starring Lon Chaney Jr, at the Princess. On our way home, one of my mates ran on ahead and hid in a dark corner of Wallgate Bridge, and as we drew level, he jumped out, screaming like a demented dervish and with claw-like hands raised above his head.

Mam nearly had some extra washing that night, and I'm not kidding.

If you walked on under this bridge and along Wallgate, there was another cinema just past Clayton Street. It was once known as Wallgate Cinema, but I always remember it being the Regal. However, it was always called the "Scratch", because, after every visit to this establishment, you were certain to be itching like mad when you came out.

The proprietress was a large, blonde lady who would dole out used comics after you'd collected your admission ticket. It was pretty noisy viewing at the

Scratch due to the amount of rambunctious kids from the close proximity of Melbourne Street and Victoria Street.

Later, the building was converted into a sewing factory and, later still, to an electroplating business.

"DO YOU REMEMBER?"

Back up Wallgate again, turn right into King Street and on to the County Playhouse, a picture house that still displays, high above the entrance, the date 1916 as the year it was built, and which is now, in this revolutionary age of change, the Ibiza night club. I think it was this cinema that first introduced a back row of double seats for courting couples.

A few yards down, on the opposite side of the road, was the Royal Court Theatre — "The Court", to us peasants. This, too, is now a night club. The Hub.

The one exceptional treat for the patrons of this cinema was the electric organ (with, I seem to remember, a one-legged organist) that would rise majestically a few feet, as he played some favourite tunes before the lights went down and in the interval.

Cross the road again to what was Lewis's Milk Bar and down King Street to the Hippodrome, which, until it burnt down in 1956, was Wigan's one and only music hall, where acts of every description did their stuff. Singing and dancing, acrobatics, and magic, and acting all before a mesmerised audience. I remember seeing *Sweeny Todd, The Demon Barber of Fleet Street*,

76

played with such an amusing twist, my ribs ached with laughing.

I also recall the Shakespeare Hotel next door. Signed photographs of every Hippodrome artist adorned the walls of every room. I often wonder where they all went to, because you can be sure of one thing, they would certainly stir many a happy memory of those bygone days.

Now just a few strides down from the "Hipp" was the Palace. As I recollect, the first entrance to the cinema was like a wide entry with a sloping "walkway" that was divided by a brown, painted wooden handrail. The walkway on the right of the rail took you to the booking office and admission tickets for the downstairs front stalls (the pit) and the back stalls. The walkway on the left of the rail was the exit one, used for leaving the cinema. To buy tickets for the upstairs (the gods) you went past the sloping walkways to the main entrance at the top of some marble steps. These seats were more expensive, but I always preferred a balcony seat, because down below I was always unlucky enough to be sat behind a tall chap with a head like a boiler, or a woman with a mop of hair like a fuzzy-wuzzy warrior.

And while we're still at the Palace, I remember a certain usher (who could have passed as an usherette) who roamed the aisles with a torch that would have put a wartime searchlight to shame, and when spotlighting some unfortunate couple in a passionate clinch, would shout out, loud and clear, "And you can cut that out, you mucky devils, or I'll have you thrown out!"

"DO YOU REMEMBER?"

Just around the corner from the Palace, at the bottom of Library Street, was the Pavilion Picturedrome — now Wigan baths. Who can ever forget that splendid ornamental frontage of the "Pav"?

Now the Pavilion was the one place where I would take my chances downstairs with the big heads and the fuzzy-wuzzies, because upstairs, on the balcony, which was always referred to as "The Monkey Rack", was not the place to be if you wanted to relax and enjoy the picture; because there were more goings-on (monkey business) than in an overcrowded zoo in the mating season.

And I always tried to get a seat on the front row close to the screen; a bit of neck ache was more preferable than having burning fag-ends, toffee papers and ice-cream tubs dropped on my head.

But our world of entertainment, the silver screens, and those (with the odd exception, of course) clean and comfortable cinemas, that could seat hundreds, were slowly, irrevocably, strangled to death by the technological advance of a square box in the corner of everyone's living room. Television!

A box that consistently, day and night, spews out so much rubbish (with deplorable plots and dialogue, and continuing streams of obscenities) that your finger hovers over the channel-changing button like a sniper with his finger on the trigger.

Even so, there is some TV material that is outstanding: some specially made for the small screen;

some, even, from the silver-screen era and some adapted from classical novels; all good, entertaining stuff. But the reliability, the consistency, just isn't there. Films of substance, plot and good acting, was once a regular, everyday occurrence; outstanding American and British films, produced in a time when Hollywood stars reigned like royalty: Bogart, Flynn, Fonda, Gable and Tracy, Dietrich, Bette Davis, Joan Crawford and a whole lot more, would, for the cost of a postage stamp, autograph and return, glossy, black and white photographs to thousands of avid fans.

And the British, too, flew the flag, with talent and pictures that proved to the Americans, and the rest of the world, that we were up there with the best.

"DO YOU REMEMBER?"

What days they were — the golden age of films. Two or three times a week of affordable enjoyment.

Aye, along King Street alone you would enter another world, a world of drama, humour, romance, horror, cowboys and Indians, song and dance. Do you remember The Ink Spots?

Now what do we have? King Street is now Binge Street, where you can get paralytic till dawn (if you last that long). Then, out you stagger, regurgitate your Happy Hour's booze in front of the club next door, and while your mates prop you up, out of this club staggers a bevy of half-naked female counterparts, who are in an even worse state than you. Saturday night and Sunday morning on the town, eh! Who would have thought that our whole way of life would disappear for ever?

We are living in a lost world: Coalmines, gone! Communities, gone! Corner shops, gone! Cotton mills, gone! Decent law-abiding pubs, gone! Cinemas, gone! An essential, unique way of life that represented all that was English, that made us a nation apart and one to be proud of Gone!

Aye, they've taken it all, but the memories of us owd uns live on. Binge Street will always be King Street, the clubs, the shopping centres, the swimming baths, will always be picture houses.

And while there are some of us still around, they will live on and on until the memories are no more.

"DO YOU REMEMBER?"

CHAPTER
SIX

The Sands of Time

FOREWORD

I have written many short stories about my upbringing, the location of my upbringing and the many unforgettable characters that I have encountered in my steady progress to manhood.

The uniqueness of our location (not far from Wigan Pier) is instilled into the very fibre of my being and indeed, gave me the inspiration to write about my, and other people's, experiences.

The canal, the railway sidings, the boneworks, the brickyard, Gambler's field, and the rundown terraces, set the scene for us, the players, in these stories. However, there is one setting that, for some reason, I have only briefly mentioned. The following story will put this oversight to rest.

Time wreaks havoc with some memories, and yet others are crystal clear, sharp and deep-set; though I must confess my recollections of our corporation cleansing department are extremely vague indeed.

The depot, that we locals called the "muck yard" was a collection of buildings consisting of stables, offices, stores, a canteen and a large assembly room for the workforce, and which were all essential for the efficient collection of rubbish, household waste and unwanted goods, that with our present day problems of climatic confusion, would be classed as recycling.

The muck yard was situated opposite the last row of terraced houses at the bottom of Mayflower Road. A high wooden-gated perimeter fence kept it secure from prying eyes and trespassers; but my family, the occupants of the end house, had a bird's-eye view from our upstairs front bedroom window.

Every year, on the first day of May, the horses were groomed to perfection, bedecked with colourful ribbons, highly-polished harnesses and gleaming brasses, and led by burnished bridles around our streets, bringing pomp and splendour to our unpretentious lives.

But the outbreak of World War Two brought change. The depot was closed and relocated, and our colourful equine parades were gone for ever.

After the war, thousands of unwanted sandbags used to protect essential buildings from enemy bombs had to be disposed of, and the area of our now non-existent muck yard was the chosen site; but for some unknown reason, the bags were emptied and the sand scattered, leaving us with an inland beach that undulated its way almost to the very edge of our murky canal, and which came to be known as the sand hills.

And this, our man-made oasis, soon became, like Gambler's Field, a multifunctional place of peace, safety and happiness, but also, on many occasions, a sheltered playground for illicit gambling, lovemaking, feats of strength and endurance, camaraderie and sportsmanship; and, as in all walks of life, a place where the intimidator and oppressor rode roughshod over the weak and less robust characters.

These bully-boys though, were overshadowed by the decent, compassionate kind, and one man who possessed these essential qualities was Jimmy "Daggie" Dagnall.

Daggie was a hard-working miner who, once above ground, breathed deep the pure air, spat out the coal dust and spent some considerable time shaking off the cramped conditions of underground labouring. In other words, Daggie was a great believer in physical fitness, though not through any of those relentless muscle-building regimens (a daily toil with pick and shovel was Daggie's regimen). No, Daggie did a few press-ups, swung his heavy Indian clubs and was a great believer in deep-breathing exercises, as recommended by T. W. Standwell of High Holborn, London. Oh, and he taught a few ragged-arsed youngsters of our dead-end paradise the noble art of that age-old sport, boxing. Because of Daggie's modest dedication, young lads (and men, too) came together as a group and came to respect, and even admire, individual strengths and weaknesses.

But if anyone was keen enough to further his ambitions, the borough's Boys' Club was just a short distance from our rough-and-ready training ground, and in exchange for a small weekly payment had every facility available for further advancement.

Two of its members were my cousin Frank, who played the bugle in the club's band, and his mate, Norman "Big Norm" Berry. Big Norm's burning ambition was to develop the most muscular body in town, and to attain this desired physique, Big Norm spent four nights a week, pushing, pulling, grunting, sweating, straining and lifting heavy iron weights.

To us flaccid, skinny weaklings, Big Norm was an envious sight to behold. His almost nude sunbathing and practised poses were a regular feature on the sand hills, and he didn't need much encouragement when asked, "Show us your muscles, Norm." And what a display as he did his "muscle dance" routine, making each and every one of them quiver, shake and bounce without even a grimace. He was so well-formed, Jack Dash, the bookie's runner, once said that the bloody lad even had muscles on his foreskin. But nobody asked him to prove it.

I admired Big Norm. To my way of thinking, anyone who would spend masochistic hours on physical development and surviving the daily temptations of everyday living must surely earn some respect for those qualities, determination, willpower and self-belief.

But even with these admirable assets, and as big as he was, Norm couldn't box. And I was a witness to this fact.

It all came to light one scorching hot Sunday afternoon, the sort of day when the sand hills drew us all like flies to a kipper: amateur boxers, gamblers, frolicking kids, the lot, and of course, Big Norm tanning his body. And me? Well, I was doing some tentative sparring under the tutorial of Daggie. My opponent was Peter "P" Clark, one of my best mates. And that's why I say tentative, because P was bigger and stronger than me and a better boxer, who, even under the watchful eye of Daggie, could rattle your teeth with some good punches.

But it was hot, very hot, and I was more than glad when Big Norm, having done enough sunbathing, strolled over to see the show. Daggie, realizing that heat and tiredness were taking over, called a halt to our lesson, and, glancing casually at Norm, said, "How about a go, Norm? Fancy your chances?"

"Nah, I don't think so; it's not my thing really."

"Scared to try, is that it?"

"I aint scared. Besides, none of them two's big enough to tackle me."

"How about me? Am I big enough?"

"I dunno. Supposin' I hurt you, what then?"

"I'll risk it. Anyway, we're having a friendly spar, not fighting for the world championship."

"Go on then, lace them on. But don't blame me."

P, helping him on with the gloves and giving me a crafty wink said, "Watch his elbows, Norm, he's a sneaky bugger, tha knows."

"His elbows? I thought we were boxin', not wrestling."

"Even so, he likes to win, and he knows all the tricks; just watch his elbows."

They made an odd pair did Daggie and Norm. Daggie down to his string vest, and pants tucked in his socks, and Big Norm down to his swimming trunks, suntanned muscles rippling, flexing and tensing with every ponderous move he made. However, his lack of combative prowess soon had him floundering against Daggie's pugilistic skill.

Actually, Daggie, because he was the compassionate type, took pity on his oversized opponent. I don't think Big Norm landed one telling blow. Daggie just back-peddled, parried, blocked and dished out a few light jabs that wouldn't have floored a decrepit nun; and a few minutes later, called time.

"Right Norm, that's enough; a few more lessons and there'll be no stoppin' you."

But me and P knew, and Daggie too, that it would never happen. And it didn't.

Now Big Norm's mate was my cousin, Frank, the only son of Auntie Mildred. Mam didn't like Auntie Mildred. I did though. Every time I passed her house on some errand or other, out she'd pop (flaming red hair lighting up the street), invite me in, give me a plate of biscuits and a glass of lemonade and see me out with a threepenny bit in my pocket and with the usual dire warning, "Don't tell your mam, Eric."

I still suffer pangs of guilt brought on by memories of those clandestine threepenny bits that Mam never knew about. Or did she? And thinking back all those years, I'm almost certain that it was Auntie Mildred's kind gestures that actually made Frank the antagonistic sod he was.

Even so, everyone knew he was a bully and a bother-maker and, in later years, carried a brass knuckleduster. But he knew when, where and with whom to make trouble. Any botheration within the confines of the Boys' Club would have meant an instant dismissal. Cousin Frank knew this and chose the time and his victims accordingly.

Frank was older than me and a stone heavier, and my first encounter with his bully-boy ways happened one Saturday afternoon while attending a funeral on the sand hills. I had borrowed Mam's coal shovel and was busy digging a hole to bury Birdy Briggs's cat that had died of dysentery the night before when up looms cousin Frank. Naturally, Birdy was a bit emotional and was blowing away at his nose and wiping the odd tear.

"What're you two playin' at, eh?" Frank demanded, then, on noticing Birdy's cat in its pillowcase shroud, he burst out laughing.

"Who's the dead un, then, eh?"

"It's Birdy's cat," I said. "We're burying him."

"A bloody cat! You're burying a bloody cat? Chuck it in t' bloody cut, you daft sods."

"No way," Birdy said. "My cat's goin' in no cut. My cat's bein' buried, proper, like."

"What difference does it make? The bloody thing's dead init?"

"I'll know the difference," Birdy said. "Besides, my mam would soddin' well kill me if I did that."

"An' I'll soddin' kill thi if tha doesn't, so take thi pick."

"Leave off, Frank; can't tha see he's upset . . . Leave him alone."

"Hey up, look who's talkin' chief gravedigger's pokin' his snotty nose in, is he?"

I decided to ignore him and began to dig into the sand again. Frank, now out of control, gave me a push, grabbed the shovel and began to backfill the hole. I made a desperate grab for his arm, he swung a fist and caught me full in the face, knocking me flat again.

"That cat's goin' int bloody canal, an' thall go wi' it, cousin!"

Birdy, now jumpy with nervous tension, began to kick sand and shout. "Leave him alone, pig, leave him alone."

Frank threw down the shovel, made a lunge for Birdy and grabbed him by the scruff of his neck.

"And what will tha do, short arse?"

At that crucially tense moment, the voice of Daggie, loud, clear and menacing, brought a stop to any further ructions, and Frank, glaring in the direction of Daggie's "school" of boxers, spat and cursed and swaggered off in the opposite direction.

Daggie's timely intervention gave Birdy and me the chance to complete the burial, but, on my suggestion, we moved the "grave" to a different spot. Knowing Frank, he would have exhumed the cat and dumped it in the canal out of spite.

On arriving home for tea, Mam, who knew I'd been giving Birdy a helping hand, wanted to know all about it.

"Well, did you lay the poor thing to rest, Eric?"

"Aye, Mam, and we said a prayer."

"Tell me another . . . you wouldn't pray over me never mind a flamin' cat."

"Honest, Mam, and Birdy were proper upset, too."

"And was he that upset that he gave you a clout?"

"A clout? What do you mean? Birdy would never clout me."

"Then who did that to your face?" She pointed to her own cheekbone below her right eye. I looked in the mirror over the mantelpiece, and, sure enough, a badly bruised cheek was plain to see.

"Oh, that . . . It were P Clark; him and a few more were doin' a bit o' sparrin', and I joined in."

"And P Clark did that to you?"

"I were just a bit slow gettin' out road, that's all."

"I thought you wore gloves."

"We do, but P can really wallop one, you know."

"I'd better have a quiet word with Daggie."

"You'd better not. I'll be the laughing stock o' Mayflower Road if you do that."

"All right then, but for God's sake learn to box proper, or you'll end-up wi' a face looking like a patchwork quilt."

And that was the end of it. Nearly.

On the following Sunday, I had just joined the usual crowd of Daggie acolytes, when the man himself took me by the arm.

"What's this I hear about you and Frank?"

"Who's been talkin', Daggie? Was it Mam or Birdy?"

"Never mind how I know; I know, and that's enough. Now get some gloves on and have a go with P."

"P?"

"Aye, P, it's time to do some serious stuff . . . Just a minute, though . . ." He paused. "Look who I've just seen."

I looked in the direction of his nod; it was cousin Frank. Daggie made a beeline for him, and a minute or two later, returned with Frank in tow.

"I've just took on a new member, Eric, and I've decided you'll be his first partner."

Frank gave me a look that spoke volumes. He was about to give me another good thumping, but this time it would be with the blessings of Daggie, all legit and above board — a legitimate assault, so to speak, and I knew I couldn't back down. If I refused to square-up to him, my self-respect and esteem would go down to zero.

The gloves were brought out. Daggie handed them to me.

"There you are, Eric, but I've changed my mind about you and Frank. He's going in with P; I think they'll make a better match."

With overwhelming relief, I gave Daggie an undying look of gratitude.

"But there is one thing you can do, Eric," he said.

"Anything."

"Help your cousin on with them gloves."

"It'll be a pleasure, Daggie."

It was a great scrap. A bit one-sided, but very enjoyable, and I still relish it to this day. P knocked the stuffing out of him, and it was only when Daggie brought a stop to Frank's punishment that I began to realize the motive behind his thinking. Daggie knew Frank didn't stand an earthly against P, and just by simply allowing me to lace on the loser's gloves, I too had played a small part in his humiliating defeat.

And time moved on, and the sand hills, like the land before, became no more. But they and what they had stood for had become part of our simple lives, and, only by remembering, still are.

'John 10'

"Do You Remember?"
A Walk For All Reasons

"DO YOU REMEMBER?"

Can you still remember those well-meaning New Year's resolutions? What were they I wonder? To go on a diet? Join a gym? Stop smoking? To save all your loose change? To be a better person and go to church? If so, are you still beavering away? Sweating, cursing, fretting and getting nowhere fast?

When I was a young un — and I could be wrong here — I never heard of anyone making a New Year's resolution. Oh, resolutions were made, that's part of life, but they didn't make owt of it. It didn't fill a page of the Daily Mail. No, they just got on with it.

There were no dramatic denials and definitely no starvation diets. Besides, most folk down our way were glad to scoff what was put in front of them. So dieting didn't exist.

I do remember one of my dad's resolutions, though. One day he decided to pack in smoking, and he sent off for this miracle cure — one month's supply of yellow, blue and brown tablets (God only knows what they consisted of). And the label read: to be taken three times a day with meals. A brown one at breakfast, a yellow one at lunch and a blue one at teatime.

So, with his fags conveniently hidden away in a cupboard, the ritual began. For two whole days that man suffered like no man should be allowed to suffer. Then he cracked! Out came the fags, and happiness once more shone like a beacon from a face wreathed in tobacco smoke.

And those miracle pills? Well, I never did find out what happened to those, but I can hazard a guess.

However, as an antidote to counteract the effects of the odd Woodbine, Dad enjoyed long country walks, which included some deep breathing, and one day, I too came to learn the benefits of this much-neglected exercise.

It was during a walk along the Leeds to Liverpool canal that I received my first lesson, which I still practise to this day.

But first we had to leave behind the stench of our boneworks and cross a wooden canal bridge, known locally (for obvious reasons) as the White Bridge, at the rear of Walker's Iron Foundary.

Once on the other side, we passed Mayflower Meadow and a stretch of tall grass near a pond edged with bulrushes, which we called "The Long Grass", a place where me and my mates, Alan Scott and Bill Gallagher, had many a frolic and a furtive fag.

We went on past these oases of pleasure towards Gathurst and the rural part of Wigan. Then Dad, breathing deep, said, "Breath in through thi nose, lad, deep and steady, like, then hold it for a few seconds, then exhale through your mouth, but make sure this lasts longer. Always empty your lungs proper; it gets rid of the impurities, understand?"

I tried and went dizzy, and my chest hurt a bit. I soon packed it in, because, for one thing, I were a bit young and giddy-like. But as I got older and wiser — although I don't think wisdom comes into it, not with me anyroad; perhaps a dash of common sense would be more appropriate — I began to realize the benefits of walking and deep breathing.

Remember, too, any doctor will tell you that the vast majority of the human race do not breath properly, they only shallow breath.

These days, I can inhale long and deep, no problem.

I don't power walk; I leave that to the young uns. I step out early mornings, six days a week, when the air is fresh and invigorating. Sometimes I walk briskly, sometimes not. As long as you're walking, why bother. My walks last an hour or more, but any walk, however short is good for you.

By the way, don't worry if you forget to deep breath, it wouldn't be enjoyable to do so continually. Do it when you feel like it. But you'll soon realize even when you're not consciously deep breathing, you'll be breathing deeper just natural, like.

So, why don't you have a go? It's good for your heart, lungs and mobility. It keeps your weight stable (you'll even lose weight if you keep at it). And it's good for the mind, because there's nothing better for beating stress. And it doesn't cost a penny.

In fact, it means, "A Walk For All Reasons".

Aye the twang of knicker-elastic and the smell of carbolic soap are now only distant memories, but the memory of what Dad taught me that day, long ago, before today's mania for gyms, health clubs and diets and unkept resolutions, will stay with me forever.

"DO YOU REMEMBER?"

CHAPTER
SEVEN

"I Could've Been Posh"

There were definitely no posh folk where I came from. Although, and I speak from experience here, when a chap bought (which wasn't often) a new pair of shoes or a suit, he did show off a bit; but he was soon deflated by many a wicked put-down.

"Hey up, here comes Lord Muck."

"What shop did thy break into, lad?"

And if his new shoes squeaked: "Are tha sure tha's paid for them?"

So you can imagine the reverberations when it came to be known that the Briggs family were about to move house. Not any old house just around the corner, but a "roses around the door" cottage in a little hamlet seven miles from Wigan's ancient borough.

And me and my family belonged to those many a flabbergasted neighbour who couldn't, or wouldn't, comprehend such a thing; but after a little prompting, Birdy Briggs himself gave me the full story.

"I've heard rumours tha leavin' country, Birdy, is it true?"

Birdy didn't even smile. "It's bloody Mam. She wants to get away . . . you know, go and live somewhere different."

"What for? You've always lived round here. What's up wi t' place?"

"She says it's a dump, and yon boneworks stinks rotten."

"It's always bloody stunk. It's a boneworks; that's why it stinks."

"I know it, you know it . . ."

"And everybody round here knows it," I said.

"Anyway, she keeps goin' on and on about me goin' to a better school, havin' a better education and a better life."

"And where is this fabulous place you're movin' to, eh?"

Birdy waved a casual hand. "I don't know for sure, somewhere int country."

"So it's true then?"

"What?"

"You're goin' to live in a cottage wi' roses for a doorway."

"I don't know for sure. I've given up listening to Mam and Dad talkin' and arguing about it all."

"But how can they afford a place like that? I mean, you need plenty o' dosh to move house."

"Well, for starters, Dad's been doin' extra shifts down t' pit, and Mam says there's a job waiting for her int post office."

"But how will your dad get to work?"

"On t' bloody bus, how do you think?"

"Oh, I thought they still had stage coaches up that way."

"Don't be a clever sod, Eric. I'm in no mood."

"Anyroad, mate, thall see plenty o' nature; you know, animals and birds . . . robins, blue tits and sky larks . . . not like round here. All you see is sparrows and rats and breathin' in the local pong."

"I still don't want to go. I bet they're all toffee-nosed sods who have a bath every night."

"And that's another thing," I said. "You'll have an inside lavvy and a bathroom and hot and cold water . . . and a bloody garden."

"How do you know that?"

"I don't for sure, but it'll still be better than livin' round here. And there's summat else."

"And what's that then?"

"Thi mam and dad might invite me up for a summer holiday."

"Cheeky bugger! Anyroad, I'm not goin' so thall not see me."

"Thall go, mate; there's no escapin' this one. If your mam and dad says so, thall go."

He did go. But the run-up to Birdy's departure was a rocky, unsettling time for everyone.

Some folk reckoned his outrageous behaviour was an act of defiance, a way of striking back at his parents for disrupting his way of life. Others said it was just an anxious cry for help, suppressed aggression coming to the surface and making him unruly and unpredictable.

Everyone became backstreet psycologists. Yes, Birdy did change, and yes, this change in character came about because Birdy was scared. Like he said, he didn't want to move. He didn't want a new life and new friends. This was where he belonged. His friends were here in Mayflower Road, not far from Wigan Pier, a rough and ready place, where knocking about with me and Richie and Picky and the rest, was a world of excitement and daring camaraderie.

His first rebellious act was a real shocker. Mrs Ashurt's toffee shop was a small place, just a converted terraced house really. She sold toffee, the odd loaf of bread, cream cakes, canned food and cigarettes. Especially cigarettes. Mrs Ashurst was not only a very likeable shopkeeper, she was our motherly confidant, a person we could trust, and of course, the supplier of our Wild Woodbine fags, that always came with a gentle warning, "Be careful, and don't tell your mam."

And it was all because of Birdy's terrible act of madness that this mutual trust and confidentiality was almost destroyed. She caught him in the very act of thievery.

At this particular time, Mrs Ashurst's doorbell wasn't working, and every honest and upright customer, as they went through the door, shouted a warning, usually, "Shop!" But Birdy didn't, did he? He entered stealthily and was helping himself to bars of Cadbury's chocolate from a display box on the counter when the old lady came through from the back and caught him red-handed.

This incident and other misdemeanours only came to light as his transgressions, fighting and vandalism continued until, finally, he went missing.

He had packed some clothing and food and had left in the dead of night; no note, no warning and, apparently, no regrets.

100

His parents went to the police station, but were told to wait awhile and call round to the homes of friends and relatives. He certainly hadn't taken refuge at our house; Mam and Dad would have chased him back in quick time.

However, as in all times of trouble, neighbours rallied round to give their loyal support, but there was no sign of him. Birdy had vanished. It was Mam who solved the mystery, really. After spending another sleepless night with Mr and Mrs Briggs, she returned home exhausted and a little overwrought.

"Do you know where that poor lad's got to, Eric?"

I was stunned and peeved by her obvious suspicions.

"Bloody hell, Mam, how should I know. Even though he is my best mate, I couldn't keep a secret like that."

"Don't swear in this house, young man . . . It were only a question." Her voice softened. "Think about it anyway. Put yourself in his shoes; where would you hide out, eh?"

I had no idea. But I did some serious thinking just the same. Where would the daft sod go? But how the hell was I to know? Birdy had just vanished into thin air. He could be dead (I shuddered at the thought), in Timbuktu or joined the Foreign Legion, even. Nobody knew owt!

That night, Mam and Dad went round to Birdy's house again, and I went to bed early. But sleep was impossible. I tossed and turned, I thought and thought, until, finally, sleep took over. Then, after what seemed only minutes, the need to urinate woke me up, and as I woke, I began to remember. I remembered the gang of us re-enacting *The Adventures of Robin Hood*. I remembered the arguments about who was to play the Erroll Flynn part of Robin, and I remembered our enactment was performed on a disused allotment down by the canal (the very same one where Cyril Meadowsweet took refuge when going AWOL nearly two years later). And suddenly I knew where Birdy was hiding out.

Mam and Dad were still round at Birdy's. I got dressed, found a torch with a very dim light and set off.

It wasn't too late, and there were still people out and about. I reached the canal towpath, which of course, proved more gloomy than our gas-lighted streets. The torch was hopeless, so I kept my eye on the canal water which reflected dimly in the darkness.

Approaching the allotment area, I began to shout Birdy's name. Even in the semi-darkness I found the allotment I wanted quite easy enough. I shouted again and began to bang on the wooden fence. Then, much to my relief, Birdy's voice came back to me, weak and uncertain, like an echo.

"Eric . . . Eric . . . I'm here, Eric . . ."

"C'mon, mate, come to the gate, hurry up!"

"Is there anybody with you?"

"No, c'mon, hurry up!"

The rattle of a chain, then the squeak of rusty hinges and he was out, standing close to me in the darkness.

"How did you know I was here, Eric?"

"Never mind that now; c'mon, we'd better get going."

"Where to? Where are we goin'?"

"You are goin' home, you daft sod, where do you think?"

"I daren't now, Eric. Mam and Dad'll kill me."

"Then all your problems'll be over, won't they, Birdy?"

"I had to get away, Eric. I had to make a stand, didn't I?"

"This won't change a thing, mate. Like I've said before, they've made up their minds and there's no escape; anyway, who knows, you might like the bloody place."

"C'mon then, let's be off. I'm bloody starvin' of hunger."

Three weeks later, at 10a.m. on Friday morning, Birdy went round to Mrs Ashurst's little shop and asked for her forgiveness, and the old lady, almost in tears by his humble act of contrition, was so overwhelmed she gave him a packet of Woodbines and a bag of Uncle Joe's Mint Balls as a going-away present.

One o'clock prompt on that same day, the Briggs trio left Mayflower Road to become a ruralised family, and I had lost one of my best mates.

For some reason or other, the house stayed empty. Perhaps it was the nearby aromatic boneworks that had persuaded would-be tenants to choose a more salubrious location. Whatever the reason, for me, the empty house was a stark reminder of Birdy and his parents. New occupants would perhaps have helped erase the memory of a respected family who had been a crucial part of a tight-knit community, which is held together with seemingly unspoken vows of honour, love, trust and compassion, and all things necessary to ease the burden of hard, penurious and troubled times.

June 1938 brought in warm and glorious weather and a stir that brought hope. The Briggs house had stood vacant for nine long months, and, like all empty houses seem to do, it had withered and wasted. However, the landlady, Mrs Ballard, with a mind like a cash register and with a possible new tenant in mind, decided to brighten the place up.

Several workmen laboured for three solid weeks, renovating inside and out and raised our hopes that new neighbours would soon be arriving.

The labouring now finished, the workmen packed up and left, and once again the house stood empty. Finally, after a few more days of further speculations, a removal van arrived. And what a welcoming sight it was. Sitting up front with the driver and his mate were Mr and Mrs Briggs, and in the back, somewhere amongst the family furniture, was my mate, Birdy, whistling his bloody head off.

Once again, Mayflower Road was buzzing with happy banter and theories: living beyond their means, lack of shops, queer neighbours, Birdy had run off again. Until, at last the true reason for their return was made known. It had been Mrs Briggs's decision. The one person who had strived so hard for a better life for her and her family just couldn't cope. To put it plain and simple, Mrs Briggs had missed the bustle of Mayflower Road, with its run-down terraced rows and the camaraderie of its occupants who gathered on the street corner, gossiping, joking and laughing, and the unlocked doors that you just tapped, entered, sat down and had tea and biscuits and a good chat about this and that and t'other. It was all of these things that had brought the Briggs family back to where they belonged. Back home.

It was a time for celebration. We had a kitty, and every gang member willingly made a donation: toffee, fags, cake and pop were purchased from Mrs Ashurst's little shop, taken down by the canal, and, in a place called Three Corner's Meadow, we had a party never to be forgotten, and afterwards, with not a swimming costume between us, headed for Paxton Locks to dive, swim and frolic like the crazy kids we were.

I was just taking a breather, treading water, slow and easy-like, when over comes Birdy, blowing and splashing and bursting with energy.

"Does tha know summat, Eric?"

"What's that Birdy?"

He prodded his bare chest with a dripping forefinger. "I could've been posh." And, chortling with glee, cocked-up his bare arse and vanished from sight.

"Do You Remember?" There Was a Time

"DO YOU REMEMBER?"

How times, and people, have changed, or should that be, how time has changed people?

I don't mean in a technological sense. Although, even in our now advanced technological world, there hasn't been any Utopian benefit, that's for sure; and it hasn't made us a better-living race of people.

Along the rocky road of progress we have lost the art of living together. Customs and conventions have suffered dramatically. People don't care much for other people any more. We are utterly swamped in a morass of self-indulgence, where a plastic card will buy you what you want and begger the consequences.

"I'm alright, Jack", is now the norm. We have now lost the true meaning of sociability, and that is why we have more social services departments than has ever been known. We have strangers being paid a wage to help us to do what "they" want, when we should be helping and caring for each other. By all accounts there are some people who don't even know the names of their next-door neighbours, even after years of living in close proximity, they are unfriendly.

So is it any wonder that almost daily we read of someone, somewhere, who has been left to fend for themselves, and even to die alone, indeed, left lying dead for days (even weeks) before the alarm is raised?

Even children have been, and are being, maltreated, even physically abused and neighbours either don't care, or pretend it isn't happening. Could it be that these same people are afraid of the consequences of intrusion? And why? Why be afraid to help someone, man, woman or child, who is suffering in one way or another?

It's a known fact that social services and the police have often failed in their duty to protect the vulnerable.

And why is it, in this age of technological progress that is supposed to make us more independent and self-sufficient, that some towns are suffering the ignominy of having "no-go areas" where even the police fear to tread? This seems to indicate that "mob rule" is prevalent. Why? What has been the cause of this abysmal downward spiral? TV violence? Lack of discipline? Our Nanny State? Unemployment?

And now, unbelievably, nurses in one hospital have signed a public pledge that they treat everyone with compassion and dignity. I was always under the impression that this was their bounden duty anyway, and that is why nurses become nurses: to nurse and give succour, compassion and tender loving care to those who are suffering ill-health, the infirmed and the dying. Surely, once they don that uniform, that is their duty.

Can there be a return to the days when people really, truly cared and had compassion and understanding for their fellow-humans?

There was a time before the ubiquitous care homes when our aged population was cared for by relatives. Most of them even passed away in their own bed, surrounded by their loved ones.

There was a time when compassionate friends and neighbours cared for the less fortunate ones.

There was a time when discipline was an accepted and approved deterrent.

There was a time when less wealth and possessions meant more generosity; not in money terms or donations, but by volunteering their time and abilities to those worse off than themselves. And their only reward was undying gratitude.

"DO YOU REMEMBER?"

CHAPTER EIGHT

Herbal Plant's Remedies

FOREWORD

To the readers of my semi-autobiographical tales, I may have been sending out the wrong messages.

In my writings I have applied diligent thought and attention to the time, the place and the many characters of my boyhood days, and because of these fond memories, I have tended to overlook some of the more spiteful and iniquitous ones. Why? I don't really know, because all of us, some more than others, have a dark side which seems to become darker and more oppressive in certain circumstances or in the company of certain people.

However, as you shall see, the influence or the misfortunes of friends or loved ones can often bring out the best of qualities in all of us.

There was no doubt about it, Herbert Plant was put on this earth to be an herbalist; an amateur one perhaps, but an herbalist just the same. Actually, there were two amateur herbalists in Mayflower Road, Herbert Plant and my dad. It was Dad's herbalist knowledge that gave Herbert the inspiration to follow in his footsteps. Often out of work, the two friends spent many hours tramping the surrounding countryside and delving into Dad's leather-bound edition of Thomas Culpeper's notable book, *Complete Herbal*, studying, cross-checking, making notes, gathering and discussing the healing qualities of those abundant wild-growing herbs.

Aye, it was these excursions and Dad's constant promptings that fashioned Herbert Plant, like Dad, into a local medicine man — no shop, no business, just word of mouth, and it was by word of mouth, too, that Herbert came to be known as "Herbal" Plant, a name that he was proud of, a name that he, in his mind's eye, could see displayed over a town centre shop window:

"HERBAL PLANT'S REMEDIES"
WALK RIGHT IN AND FIND A CURE

And this was the crux of the matter. Herbal's growing knowledge and application of successful treatments made him a tad too cocky. Arguments with Dad, our professional and established herbalist, Isaac Greenwood and even Doctor Merry became a regular occurrence, and, inevitably, led to a manic quest for self-improvement.

He spent hours in the library's reference room and borrowed books from the lending department. But it wasn't just a knowledge in the field of herbalism that Herbal pursued; he suddenly saw himself as a possible authority on a vast range of subjects which included, psychology, sociology and philosophy.

111

But in his self-centred, ardent pursuit of worldly wisdom, Herbal had overlooked one thing: his nemesis — his wife.

Ada Plant was small in stature, dark, grim and formidable, her attention to detail, housework and cleanliness was matchless. A childless, pocket-rocket housewife and cleaner, whose relentless scrubbing and polishing drove Herbal insane. She didn't drink and was a regular church-goer and could make a good wholesome meal from almost nothing. Her acid tongue, though, condemned Herbal's accomplishments to all and sundry: neighbours, rent collector, gas meter reader, milkman, the lot.

Just like the rest of Mayflower Road, their terraced house had two bedrooms. Ada and Herbal shared a bed in the front one, and the backroom was Herbal's workroom where he dried his herbs and mixed his balms and potions. This room was Herbal's sanctuary, a place to escape from Ada's virulent condemnations.

She allowed Herbal to "play at doctor" for one reason only; her sister, Hilda, a spinster who lived in Hurrydown Lane, had once suffered a badly strained and bruised ankle which Herbal treated and cured after only one week. And indeed, this early success had paved the way for Dad's friend in an age when assistance and compassion for one's neighbour was a regular, unasked-for occurrence.

Bob Woolley was worried, and when Bob Woolley was worried, Bob Woolley usually got drunk. That's how desperate Bob Woolley was. And for an answer to his problem, Bob made a beeline for the Three Crowns public house and the company of Herbal Plant.

"Can I buy you a drink, Herbal?"

"That's reet good o' you, Bob. What's the occasion? Is it a win on t' pools, or what?"

"That'll be the day."

So, with foaming glasses and a salutary chink of "cheers", the duo retired to a vacant corner, and, after a ten-minute mutual attack on a few government policies, Bob changed the subject.

"What do you think o' Doctor Merry, Herbal?"

"If you mean, is he a good doctor, well, he's as good, if not better, than some I've heard of. Why?"

"It were only a question."

"He's never treated me for owt at all. I does my own doctorin'."

"And other folks too, that I do know, Herbal."

Herbal, pleased with Bob's comment, gave his friend's knee a matey tap.

"You're not havin' problems, are you, Bob?"

Bob, slightly flustered, said, "Me? No, no, course not." He drained his glass. "Sup up, Herbal, and have a refill."

"Hang on, it's my turn. I'll get these."

But Bob was already heading for the bar. And that's when Herbal knew for sure that Bob had a problem. Bob returned, sat down, took a long deep drink, and said, "There is summat, Herbal . . . and I was wonderin' . . ." He broke off, looking slightly embarrassed.

"C'mon, man, what is it? It's not down below, is it?"

113

"Bloody hell, Herbal, there's nowt wrong wi' that lot."

"What's wrong then? Spit it out, man."

"Well, it's the wife, actually."

"Your Betty?"

"Aye. Well, you know we've got a reet sizeable brood, don't you?"

"How many is it, seven?"

"That's it, seven, and she's ended up wi' a bunch o' piles to prove it."

"Women wi' plenty o' kids usually have, Bob."

"But she's sufferin', Herbal, an' it's affecting everything she does, everything, if you know what I mean."

"Has she been to see Doctor Merry?"

"She has, an' that were a waste o' time; he gave her some ointment, but it were useless."

"Give me a couple o' days, Bob, an' I'll sort it out."

"There's just one thing though, Herbal."

"What's that?"

"Can we keep this secret-like? If she finds out I've been talkin', she'll kill me."

"No problem. Tell her you've been to see Isaac Greenwood."

"Thanks pal . . . Now c'mon, sup up, and I'll get you another."

Two weeks later, all of Mayflower Road knew of Bob Woolley's "secret". His wife's obvious cure could be contained no longer, and Herbal's apparent knowledge of herbal remedies amazed us all. Even Dad, who also knew a thing or two, was proud of him, and after a little subtle probing, confirmed his own ideas as to his friend's cure.

"Lesser Celandine, was it, Herbal?"

"That it were, mate, that it were, and you know as well as I do it's also called "Pilewort" because the roots have a look of piles about them, but I don't need to tell you, do I?"

"I can see you've done your homework," Dad said. "But did you know that Wordsworth himself even had the name carved on his tomb."

"Oh, aye?"

"Aye, and it goes summat like this: 'THERE'S A FLOWER THAT SHALL BE MINE; 'TIS THE LITTLE CELANDINE'."

"I didn't know that, you clever bugger," Herbal said.

And as time went on, Herbal's many cures (all free, of course) earned him an enviable reputation. But as his status among us locals grew, he became extremely discerning and chose his "patients" accordingly. He had this uncanny sense of knowing who would respond to his healing ways, and to overcome any self-doubts, he would have certain remedies prepared and ready for anyone who would respond to his treatments.

Among his favourites was "nettle tea", a concoction that was guaranteed to cure or alleviate and relieve, among other things, gout and bronchitis and was best known as a tonic to enrich the blood.

Aye, according to today's rich and varied, but sometimes baffling language, Herbal was on a roll. His fame grew, his ego, too . . . until . . . Ada Plant could stand it no longer. As she sank deeper into a bog of despondency, her vindictive, cruel nature which was always with her, began to simmer and boil. His success; that upstairs room, smelling strongly of drying herbs; his laziness; his laughing, joking friends; all of these things, and more, stirred up the bile and bitterness that had been simmering for so long.

They had just dined on Lancashire hotpot and red cabbage, a meal that always left Herbal replete and contented. A moment of peaceful quiet prevailed, then the shock . . .

"I want you out of that front room, Herbert."

Herbal couldn't believe it. But he knew by the tone of her voice that she meant it. He knew and had suffered from the cruelty of Ada's actions before, but this!

"Did you hear me, Herbert?"

"But why, Ada? I need that room for my work."

"Work! Work! You don't call that work, collecting a few stalks and flowers and roots and serving them up to your friends who think they're sick? Come off it, Herbert."

"But why? I've always used the room; surely you don't need it for anything."

"That's were you're wrong, Herbert. I am going to use it . . . I'm taking in a lodger."

"A lodger? But why?"

"Because the money will come in handy, and the house will look like a house again."

"Aye, a bloody lodging house."

"Don't swear at me, Herbert Plant. Anyway, it's all arranged."

"And who is this lodger? Where's he from? What does he do? How do you know he's not some kind of villain?"

"He'll be suitable, because I've asked Father Dillon to find me a nice, quiet, respectable gentleman."

"Father Dillon?"

"Yes. The church has always helped the homeless, or those looking for work, people who need help to settle and find themselves, so to speak."

"So Father Dillon's going to plonk the perfect lodger on us, is he?"

"That's right. I trust his judgement, and I trust you to abide by my decision . . . you can begin clearing out that room as soon as you like."

"Why are you doing this to me, Ada?"

"Because I'm going to have a house again, not a smelly two-bit herbalist shop."

"But it's only one room — a room you don't even use."

"All that is about to change, Herbert, and the sooner you get cracking, the sooner I can begin the preparations."

Ada's decision had a catastrophic effect on Herbal, and in an attempt to ease his anguish, he told Dad his tale of woe.

"I wouldn't do anything just yet, Herbal," Dad said.

"But she's pushing me, mate. She's demanding I make a start as soon as possible."

"Tell her you want Isaac Greenwood to have your herbs, and he's making room for them."

"Knowing Ada's mind, she'll not buy that story."

"Try anyway."

"There is one thing I could try," Herbal said.

"What's that?"

"I could try givin' her a dose of hemlock."

Dad laughed. "Now you don't mean that."

"Oh, yes, I do."

"Just do as I say," Dad said. "And I'll call on Father Dillon an' see where he's up to." He gave Herbal a wink. "Who knows: he may be having problems getting someone suitable, if you know what I mean."

But Ada was fast losing patience and began to pester the priest even more. And it worked. He even brought the would-be lodger with him. But Ada wouldn't invite them in. Like she said to her ecstatic husband, "Just imagine, Herbert — a woman! And not even a presentable one, either . . . Standing there on our doorstep, puffing away on a cigarette, a tatty fur coat on her back and make-up that had been put on with a trowel; she looked a right trollop. God knows what our neighbours would have thought. I'm really disappointed with Father Dillon, I really am."

"You can't blame him, Ada. I mean there's all kinds of folk seeking help from the church; they can't pick and choose. That wouldn't be fair."

"Ah well, we'll manage as we are, thank you very much . . . Just imagine!" She gave an involuntary shudder.

Herbal soon came knocking on our front door, and after giving Dad this "unbelievable, incredible, fantastic, smashing, terrific" news, said, "You don't seem surprised. How come?"

118

"I told you to bide your time, didn't I? And look what's happened."

"Aye, an' you said summat else as well."

"Did I?"

"Aye, you said you were goin' to call on Father Dillon, an' look what did happen, you crafty bugger."

However, Ada, being the bitter, unreasonable person she was, was soon giving Herbal the daily aggravation he didn't deserve; indeed, her barbed, malicious remarks seemed to grow in strength, forcing Herbal to spend more and more time in his self-styled herbarium room.

Once again, the tension and discomfort was getting almost unbearable, and Herbal's mood darkened into despondency once again.

There seemed to be no end to this stressful situation, until one day, quite by chance, hope returned in the guise of Hilda, Ada's sister.

Ada loved her sister dearly, of that, there wasn't any doubt, and her frequent visits to Hilda's home in Hurrydown Lane were appreciated by all concerned, especially Herbal. Then came the change. Ada would return home with an increasingly worried expression on her bird-like countenance, and one day, unable to contain herself any longer, all was revealed, and with the revelation came a softening of Ada's harshness.

"I think our Hilda's losing her mind, Herbert."

"In what way, Ada?"

"She keeps on repeating herself, and she's cleaned that flamin' bird cage out three times while I've been there."

"She's got a touch of dementia, that's all."

"A touch? Uh! I think it's more than a touch."

"We all do odd things as we get older, Ada."

"Don't be daft; she's not that old."

"Some folk start early, you know."

"It goes deeper than that. T' other day she asked when our mam was calling round."

"But your mother's been dead for donkey's years."

"Exactly."

"Do you want me to have a walk round?"

"You keep away from my sister. You're a tin-pot herbalist, not a brain surgeon."

"I didn't mean it that way."

"So you don't believe what I'm telling you?"

"Course I do, I just thought . . ."

"Don't think, Herbert, things are bad enough."

And they got worse. One Sunday teatime, Hilda went missing, and a panic-stricken Ada, who had gone round to check on her, alerted the street. Eventually, she was found sitting by the canal waiting for a friend who, as Ada knew, had emigrated to America and had been living there for the last 20 years.

That was the last straw for Ada. The next day she went round to her sister's house, rearranged a spare bedroom, ordered a gladdened Herbal to help with some removals — clothes, bedsheets, food and other odds and ends that women like to have about them — and moved in to become her sister's full-time carer.

And Herbal? Well, what more could a man, who had been a victim of her venomous tongue and unforgiving ways, ask for?

120

There was not a happier person in Mayflower Road, and when Ada did call to do his cleaning, washing and ironing, Herbal made a diplomatic retreat to his makeshift herbarium room, to potter around, to breath deep those smelly drying herbs and perhaps, just perhaps, prepare a few more HERBAL PLANT'S REMEDIES.

"Do You Remember?"
The Power of No

"DO YOU REMEMBER?"

Apart from the various connotations of the word NO, it is when used in the context of denial or refusal that it becomes most powerful and, often, the most hated.

But should it be used more often as a disciplinary word? Have we lost, or forgotten, the advantages of saying NO?

Surely today's children, with their obsessions for possessions, wealth and fame, would benefit if parents (and grandparents) made better use of the word and its true meaning.

Is there a link between its lack of use and the inevitable rise of violence, cruelty and dishonour?

Is the lack of use turning our children into monsters? Are we, as elders, overeager in our willingness to please and placate the young ones?

Would using the word NO more often, make our children (and their children) better people? Were we a better and a more compassionate race of people when we had nowt and had nowt to give? Were they better days when money was scarce? When purses and dented money boxes were scrutinized and fretted over? When we didn't know which way to turn? When buying one thing meant not buying another? When children often heard the word NO and ran off to play and to ask another day?

Gone are the days when the word of a parent was law and was accepted as such. Kids were kids and tantrums were thrown, but house rules were abided by.

It was usually left to Mother to lay down the law, and Dad, sitting in his fireside chair, buried his head deeper into his newspaper and said nowt. Unless, of course, a firmer, sterner and a more threatening attitude was deemed essential.

And do dads nowadays use their disciplinary powers as "Master" of the house (and their children) like they did in times gone by? The late night predatory, feral gangs who play havoc with honest, law-abiding folk, seem to indicate otherwise.

Back then, in penurious times, before plastic money cards and ISAs and loans and the omnipresent cars and televisions, people lived within their means. They had their wants, but they were necessary wants, when the choice was perhaps a pair of shoes or a Sunday roast, when a disused tea caddy held the household savings, which the kids knew about, but never opened.

It was a time when Dad, who had a few coppers left over from his weekly "pocket money", gave it back to his grateful "Bank Manager" — his wife. A wife who knitted and sewed and crocheted and worried and said

NO to her ever demanding family, who knew that word so well and (reluctantly, perhaps) accepted it, because she was boss.

So, are modern parents as strong as they used to be? Would our children be better children and less demanding if they heard and respected that small, but powerful word NO, more often?

"Can I go out?"

"NO!"

"Can I watch tele?"

"NO!"

"Can I have this . . . and that . . . and t' other?"

"NO! NO! NO!"

Just imagine the impact.

And there's something else, too, about that word, NO! It gives the enforcer of that word a certain "boost", a feeling of doing right.

And would we be a happier, slimmer, fitter race of people if we all said NO more often?

It could even help control the world's ever increasing population. Maybe, maybe not, but the advantages are limitless.

It's a debatable, challenging subject that would perhaps make an interesting, thought-provoking, Sunday morning television programme.

"DO YOU REMEMBER?"

CHAPTER
NINE

Valentine Days

As I've mentioned before in an earlier story, Mayflower Road was a long road that only became "ours" once you passed under a low railway bridge and into "our" world; the sand hills, the brickyard, the railway sidings, the boneworks, Gambler's Field, the canal and onwards into the countryside; quite literally, a world of adventure.

Harry Valentine was nondescript, a teenager with no outstanding features, an "ish" lad, tallish, thinnish and with reddish hair. He was an altar boy at St Joseph's Catholic church, and his mother, who never missed his 10 o'clock Sunday morning mass, glowed with pride as he, dressed in crisp, virginal white vestment that seemed to highlight his reddish hair into a ginger halo, performed his acolyte duties.

The more Harry kept away from us, the harum-scarums, the better she liked it, and at seventeen years of age, she drew comfort from the fact that he was the oldest and most respected of all the acolytes. Being an only son, he was, naturally, a mother's boy. Painfully shy and nervous, he would hesitate before following anyone's lead just in case it amounted to something sinful or against his principles. He was, and always had been, just a casual gang member. Never fully committed, he would fade into the background or make some excuse to return home if things became too rambunctious. His only pastimes were reading, visiting the library to browse and explore and listening to the radio.

And that sums up Harry Valentine. Shy, committed to his church and something of a loner, a lover of literature and the calm of the library, flicking through the card-index system and breathing in the odour of books. In fact, the library was a place comparable to his church with its own distinctive pungent aroma of incense and, of course, the hallowed atmosphere.

Although his father was somewhat sceptical of his son's lifestyle, his mother's approval was all that mattered. But fate, destiny, chance, call it what you will, comes calling in many guises, and Harry Valentine's came along in the shape, form and name of Jennifer Marshalls. She, too, lived in Mayflower Road, at the top end, the more quieter part, well away from our foul smelling boneworks.

Blonde, petite and blue-eyed, she also attended church, a protestant one, the church of St Thomas, just a prayer away from St Joseph's. And she too, loved literature, and that's how she and Harry met, one Saturday morning amongst those literary giants, Dickens and H. G. Wells.

They didn't speak, but Harry consumed with excited curiosity, couldn't get her out of his mind.

The following Saturday, they met again. Same time, same spot, but this time Harry did a very daring thing; furtively, he watched and waited and bided his time and followed her outside, and Jennifer didn't miss a trick. Streets ahead in wit and wile, she put her plan into motion.

Harry, just a yard or so behind, saw the girl stumble, drop her books and leaning heavily against the library wall, put a hand to her forehead. Harry, nervous, apprehensive, but gallant to the core, moved in.

"Are you alright?"

In a voice that would have put Bette Davis to shame, she acknowledged Harry's concern.

"Yes . . . yes . . . I think so . . . thank you . . ." She touched her head again. "It was just a dizzy spell. I feel really stupid."

Harry collected her books.

"Take some deep breaths; that usually works."

"I'll be fine in a few minutes . . . Thanks anyway for your concern."

Now emboldened, our reckless hero took her gently by the elbow.

"It's better if I walk with you a bit . . . If you don't mind, that is."

"That's very good of you, thanks again."

He handed her the retrieved books.

"Can you manage?"

He steered her along the pavement. His mind was racing. With the crisis now over, he was running out of words.

"Er, do you have a bus to catch?"

"No, no, I don't live very far. I'm very nearly a neighbour of yours, actually."

"A neighbour?"

"Yes, I live in Mayflower Road."

"You do? I've never seen you."

"We live right at the top. I've seen you . . . once or twice, anyway."

"Probably when I've been going into town or to the library, perhaps."

"My name's Jennifer "Jen" Marshalls."

"And I'm Harry Valentine."

"Ooh! What a lovely, romantic name."

Harry blushed. "Do you think so?"

"I do, yes. Has no one ever told you?"

"No, and I can't see any of the lads saying owt like that, can you?"

Jennifer giggled. "Don't you have a girlfriend?"

"No, never had one."

"Where do you work?"

"I don't."

"You don't? Are you that well-off?"

"Wish I was. I used to work for Letman's, you know, the dairy people?"

"And what happened?"

"I fell out with Mr Letman over some overtime he owed me, so I packed it in."

"That's where I work; why don't you try there?" She pointed to a factory with a tall chimney and the name BLAKES MILL set into the grimy structure in white tile-faced bricks.

"Blakes Cotton Mill. Is that where you work, then?"

"It's noisy, it's dusty and it's hard work, but beggars can't be choosers."

"They won't take me on. In another few months the army'll be after me."

"National Service?"

"That's it. King and country and all that business."

A few minutes later, they turned the corner into Mayflower Road. They stopped in front of number 20.

"This is where we live, with my auntie Alison."

"We?"

"Me and my sister, Mary; she's older than me. She works at Blakes too."

"You've not far to travel, anyway."

"You'll have to come round for tea sometime and meet them both."

And giving him one of her specially practised, slow, lingering smiles, she went indoors.

A now smitten Harry was in a quandary. He had to see her again, of that, there was no doubt. He had never before in his sheltered life had such an experience. To meet, assist and converse for so long with someone of the opposite sex, who had the same interests in literature and was a fantastic looker, was just unbelievable, and best of all, she seemed to have taken a liking to him.

But how? The top end of Mayflower Road seemed miles away. He couldn't just go marching up to her front door and ask for her, could he? And he couldn't keep walking up there with an almost futile chance of bumping into her like the library one. His heart skipped a beat. That was it! The library. But how long had she borrowed her books for? A week? A fortnight? Was she a fast or slow reader? Did she visit the library at the same time on Saturdays? He had to know. After all that's how they had met, on consecutive Saturday mornings. He couldn't wait.

That morning, the books, the titles, were just a blur as his eyes darted here, there and everywhere, between shelves, across the aisles and around corners.

"Hello, Harry." From behind, her mellifluous voice almost floored him.

He tried to keep calm and nonchalant.

"Hi, I didn't see you there."

"I've only just arrived."

"Oh. Are you alright? I mean, have you had any more dizzy spells?"

"Not a one. I was telling Auntie Alison and our Mary about you and what you did."

"I didn't do anything, really."

"You did and all, and my auntie says you must be a gentleman . . . and those are hard to come by round these parts."

Harry, unable to contain himself any longer, said, "Would you like to go out with me?"

"On a date, you mean?"

Sweating and blushing profusely, he became apologetic. "I mean, that's if you want to . . . you might have a boyfriend already . . . I hope . . ."

"I don't, and if you want me to become your girlfriend, I will."

Harry smiled with relief.

"How about one night next week?"

But Jen wasn't hanging about.

"How about tonight?"

And being the gentleman Jen's Auntie Alison said he was, he took her to the pictures, best seats (paid for by his anxious mother), and taking his first date ever so seriously, he made sure it was a previous box office hit, called *Gone with the Wind*.

In the intermission, he bought her a tub of ice cream, after which, she gave his hand an encouraging squeeze and kept a firm, possessive grip until the film was over. A peck at her doorstep and Harry knew he was in love, especially when she invited him for tea the next day.

"But what about your Auntie Alison?"

"I've already asked her."

"By 'eck, that were quick!" thought Harry.

And it was over tea that Harry learned that Jen, too, went to church every Sunday. Not his church, but the protestant church of St. Thomas's.

That night, a worried Harry told his already anxious mother about his unease.

"And have you told her about being an altar boy?"

"No, Mam. I think she might pack me in if I do."

"Does she know you're a Catholic?"

"I don't want to lose her, Mam."

"Think of the consequences, lad. You a Catholic altar boy and she a protestant — there'll be hell to pay."

"Anyway, it's time I gave it all up. I'll be in the army before long."

"If you pass your medical. And what about Father Dillon? Even if you give up being a server, you're still a Catholic, and you know what he's like."

"He won't find out."

"He will! He has more spies on the ground than Stalin."

And she was right. Informers told Jen's Auntie Alison, Father Dillon and Mrs Valentine, too, about that great divide that was so persistent in those early days of religious bigotry.

Everyone, except Jen's sister, Mary, were against this seemingly doomed relationship. But these threats and condemnations did nothing to quell their regard for each other. Even when Jen's auntie confronted her with confirmation of Harry's religion and acolyte duties, they clung together.

Bike rides to the seaside resort of Southport, visits to the cinema and countryside rambles all seemed to consolidate their love for each other.

It was on one of these romantic country excursions that Jen, lying beside Harry in deep, lush, green grass, looked up at a powder-blue sky and said, all dreamy-like, "Just imagine, Harry, one day I might be Jennifer Valentine. How lovely. Valentine you, Valentine me, Valentine days. What a wonderful thought."

But Jen and Harry's romantic notions came to an abrupt stop. Harry passed his medical and within weeks was doing his basic training at Park Hall Camp, Oswestry.

But their letters bore witness to their undying love for each other and, as if to confirm the contents of those letters, each envelope was sealed and signed with the acronym SWALK: Sealed With A Loving Kiss.

Could it have been these visible indications of those two besotted romantics, and of course bigoted intolerance, that finally convinced Auntie Alison to take action? Or was it a joint conspiracy between her, Father Dillon and Harry's mam, that eventually came between a couple of young lovers cruelly separated by circumstances beyond their control?

His basic training now over, Private Valentine was posted to Aldershot for a spell of more intensive soldiering. And a later posting saw him at an army petroleum depot a few miles from Bournemouth, where he was ordered to report to the officer's mess as an assistant barman to a veteran soldier who was about to return to civvy street.

This army life, the discipline, the camaraderie and now a job mixing and serving alcoholic drinks, had changed Harry from a shy, underweight, altar boy to a robust, confident and extroverted man, a man to be reckoned with. But even so, like all servicemen, Harry looked forward to writing and receiving his weekly mail, to and from home. But when Jen's letters became less frequent and briefer in content and with SWALK too, now omitted, he began to get worried.

Then, one day he received a letter from Mary, Jen's sister.

"Dear Harry

I had to write. Our Jen is seeing someone else. Actually he's in hospital. His name is Stan Thomas; he works at Blakes with Jen and me, and he had this accident. He was biking to work, and a lorry collided with him, and he ended up in hospital, so me and Jen thought we'd pay him a visit to cheer him up because he's going to be there for a long while yet. Well, that was the start, because our Jen's never been away since, sitting there, holding his hand . . . she makes me sick. Trouble is, Auntie Alison is egging her on. I think she has it in for you, Harry, with you being a Catholic and all. Anyway, I'm sorry it's bad news, but I had to write, because it is only fair that you should know what's going on.

Love Mary x"

Harry didn't reply to Mary's letter, and he still wrote almost daily to Jen without a mention about her new-found love.

He was now due for his first seven days' leave, and, wanting a face-to-face with Jen, he played crafty. Without any prior warning to Jen or his mother, he arrived home very early one morning and, after reassuring his mother that he hadn't gone AWOL, went to bed.

After a slap-up tea, Harry, still in uniform, went along Mayflower Road and knocked on Jen's front door. It was Jen herself, dressed and ready for the street, who answered his knock.

The shock, the confusion, the guilt, were all quite obvious and, for Harry, very satisfying.

"Harry!"

"Hello, Jen. Going somewhere?"

"Yes, I am really. I'm off to visit a friend in hospital."

"Friend or boyfriend?"

Jen blushed.

"I know our Mary wrote to you. She told me all about it."

"Why didn't you tell me Jennifer? Why leave it to someone else to do your dirty work? And why let your Auntie Alison take over your life?" He raised his voice. "Can you hear me Auntie Alison? Eh? Can you hear me?"

"It's no good shouting, Harry; she's not in. Besides, it won't change a thing. As soon as Stan's out of hospital, we're getting married."

Just then, Mary came to the door.

"I thought it was you, Harry. Are you alright?"

"Aye, now I know for sure what's goin' on . . ."

Jennifer pushed past him.

"I've got to go now, Harry. I'm going to be late." She touched the sleeve of his uniform. "I'm sorry, Harry, very sorry."

As she hurried away, Mary invited him in for a drink.

"Thanks all the same, Mary, but I'd better be off." He glanced at his wristwatch. "Besides, I think it's just about opening time at The Three Crowns alehouse."

"Has she told you they're getting married and that they're coming to live here?"

"It's going to be a bit crowded, isn't it?"

"I'm moving out; a friend of mine has a place t'other side of town. I'm moving in with her."

"Good for you, Mary."

"What I can't understand is that Auntie Alison's not all that fond of men really, and she'll definitely not like Stan Thomas."

136

"Oh. Why not?"

"Well, our Jen's not told her yet, but, just like you, Stan's a Catholic, too."

And Harry, with a broad smile said, "Poor Jen. She's found a Catholic and lost a Catholic, and she's lost her VALENTINE DAYS."

John '10

"Do You Remember?"
I Kid You Not

"DO YOU REMEMBER?"

Once again we are a nation under threat. Not from foreign lands. Not from despotic tyrants, but from our own kind, the bureaucratic kind, who have systematically undermined and destroyed our very own concepts of what is right and what is wrong by imposing upon us, idiotic schemes that are supposedly meant to improve our way of life.

These blinkered do-gooders have attacked and are slowly, irrevocably, destroying a way of life that has been part of our island's proud tradition for centuries.

Almost every day, someone, somewhere, is making a decision, not from grass-roots experience or some infinite knowledge, but from their own dogged, wilfully misguided personal point of view, a point of view which challenges all reasoning and common sense. These so-called modern legislators have brought (and continue to bring) misery, confusion, frustration and chaos to a British, unique way of life that was once the envy of the world.

★　★　★

Not satisfied with promoting obscure, confusing laws for this, that and t'other way to restrict our age-old freedom of speech and choice, they now use our schools to further their war against common-sense values.

"Pupil Power" is a scheme which has been introduced to certain schools where they, the pupils, have been given the ultimate powers (and the right) to select their own brand of teacher.

These educated, conscientious people are put on "trial" by a bunch of school kids, whose ridiculous, probing and interrogation methods gives them the right to decide who has the right to teach them. And just to make the whole concept of this scheme more selective and responsible, these minor-inquisitors can report their findings to a higher authority.

These children have been given the powers to destroy a mature, intelligent person's chance of a teaching post by submitting them to a barrage of ridiculous, infantile questions that don't even relate to the educational requirements and are subsequently meant to embarrass and demean someone with more nous than themselves.

As a result, one teacher was labelled "Humpty Dumpty" and another was asked to sing her favourite song, and, when she refused, she wasn't selected.

So what next? Even if our bureaucratic know-alls don't promote these school children to the status of "Pupils over Parents" (you never can tell), these kids now have the confidence and the audacity to use these new-found powers on Mum and Dad. If they can legally undermine the rights of the teaching profession, why not try some dictating at home? Why not interrogate Mum about her household duties? Why are they being told what to do and what not to do? If they can take control of the own schooling why not their own upbringing

To hell with discipline too! Power is a wonderful thing!

And what about our future generations? What about the children of those children who have taken control of their own lives? It all stems from leniency and a lack of discipline. Let the bully take control, and he'll make your life hell.

But what price school authority and obedience? A recent newspaper report highlighted a court case over a case of assault: a teacher allegedly slammed down a Pritt Stick tube and stood accused of injuring a disruptive pupil's thumb. A hospital had already dismissed the injury as superficial. But the case went on at a cost of £30,000 a day, against a decent lady with 30 years of teaching experience. Thankfully, the case was dismissed

There was a time when respect for authority, people and property was an accepted asset on the way to adulthood. There was a time when the term "Love thy neighbour" and "Love thy Father and thy Mother" were infinite words of wisdom. Ancient, perhaps, but still crucially essential in a modern world.

No one wants a return of the fist and cane type of discipline, but common sense must surely prevail.

Discipline is (or should be) part of life, a part of growing up. Question, by all means, ulterior motives, but with our present day obsession with laxity and the eliminating of authority in schools and homes, then we are on a slippery slope of no return.

"DO YOU REMEMBER?"

CHAPTER
TEN

A Stool Pigeon's Revenge

Even in those desperate times of poverty, the public house was an oasis, set not in a sea of sand, but in strategic (and numerous) places of dereliction, where landlords collected weekly rents and left their tenants cussing loudly at their lack of care and repair.

Now a pub landlord was different. They (most of them, anyway) felt it their bounden duty to keep customers happy and contented.

But running a pub means sacrifice. Life would never be the same again, and you've got to learn fast. You have to play many parts, and yet stay neutral: a pacifier, an in-between man, a sympathizer, who, like a Catholic priest taking a confessional, gives his blessings and yet keeps his silence.

The Three Crowns alehouse was Eddie and Ethel Black's first. This was new territory for them, and they were keen to make an impression (and a living) from this new and exciting venture.

Earlier, introductory visits to the pub and its departing landlord, Benny Burnside, had been enlightening and instructive. A slate with a record of debts still owed by three of his customers was brought to their attention.

"That particular chap, Alf Jimson — you'll definitely have to watch him," Benny said. "He works down t' pit, when he goes that is. I remember once, he paid Doctor Merry a visit complaining about dust on his lungs, but the doc kicked him out. 'The only dust you've got on your chest is from scraping burnt toast,' he told him."

"And are there any more rum-uns we should know about?" Eddie said.

"I can't tell you everything; there's things you've got to find out yourselves and in your own way."

"That's fair enough, Benny."

"There is somebody, though, I think you should know about."

"Oh?"

"Sergeant Welsby; he's strict, stringent and unscrupulous, is Welsby. he's a bugger."

"I thought all policemen were like that."

"Not like Welsby, they're not. He makes his own rules and plays the game his way, if you know what I mean . . . And he'll be calling in on you to see what you're made of."

"Thanks for the warning; we appreciate it."

"As I said, you'll find things out as you go along, things that'll make you wonder what's what and who's who."

Just one week after moving in, Eddie and Ethel began to make changes. The slate was wiped clean. A new dartboard was put in place. The piano was retuned, and a regular pianist, Philip "Sid" Sidney was hired, and, not to be outdone by local clubs, Eddie advertised for male and female vocalists.

144

And even Ethel came up with a gem of an idea.

"How about forming a ladies dart team, Eddie?"

"Women throwing darts . . . That's a new one."

"I know it is, but times are changing, Eddie; we're getting more liberal minded since the war, us women."

"Well, it's never been done before, not round here, anyway, so it just might take off. Who knows?"

"We'll never know if we don't try, and while we're at it, I appoint myself captain of the team."

"You? You can't throw darts."

"Then I'll have to get in plenty o' practice, won't I?"

So, prior to organizing her team, "The Three Crowns Darters", Ethel, behind closed doors, practiced and practiced until her arm ached and her skill became such that no one could deny her the rightful status as captain of the team.

He called one Sunday evening, did sergeant Welsby. A knock on the small serving-hatch window in the passageway had Eddie thinking it was some kid wanting pop or crisps, and he went over to serve only to find the uniformed figure of Welsby waiting to greet him.

"Mr Black, is it?"

"That's me, and you're Sergeant Welsby, I assume."

"Right first time . . . Could we have a little tête-à-tête in your living room, sir?"

Leaving Ethel in charge of the bar, Eddie took him through. He removed his helmet to reveal a sparse head of hair, and his face glowed healthily. He lowered himself into a fireside chair.

"Quiet tonight."

"Usually is on a Sunday . . . Tea?"

"No, thanks; next time, perhaps."

"You're always welcome, Officer."

"There's going to be a raid on your pub, Mr Black, and I'll be using your premises to apprehend the criminals."

Dumbstruck, Eddie stared at him in disbelief.

"Not a raid on your takings, nothing quite so dramatic, I'm afraid." He sounded disappointed.

"What other kind of raid is there?" Eddie said.

"A bottle-snatching raid, sir."

Eddie burst out laughing.

"A bottle-snatching raid? Is this some joke, or what?"

"I never joke when it comes to criminality, sir."

"Then you'll have to explain, Sergeant."

"It's kid's stuff, really. There's a certain gang of local roughnecks who, under the cover of darkness, scale your yard wall, remove the bottom layer of empty bottles from your stacked beer crates and, at a later date, bring them back to your pub for money on the returns."

"It's not exactly robbing the Bank Of England, is it?"

"It's thieving, Mr Black, and entering your premises illegally."

"But it's only coppers, surely . . ."

Welsby raised a hand.

"That's how it all starts, a bit here, a bit there, and before you know it, they're robbing for real."

"And how did you find out about this?"

"From here, from this public house."

For the second time that night, Eddie was speechless.

"I have an informer, who is also one of your customers, sir."

"Who is it?"

"Now, now, sir, that's a foolish question. I can't tell you that, can I?"

"Why not? It's my pub. I have every right to know what's going on, and who this person is."

"This person is doing essential police work, and I have every right to keep his identity concealed, sir."

"But how the hell did he come to know about a few penniless lads keen to make a shilling or two?"

Welsby shrugged.

"He also keeps me informed about the rampant stealing of coal from the railway sidings, and I've made a few arrests in that quarter, too."

"He's a right little stool pigeon, isn't he?"

"I prefer to call him an informer."

"You would, but it's the same difference; he's sold his soul to the devil."

"So I'm the devil, am I?"

"The devil, a policeman, whatever, but if I find out who this . . . stool pigeon is, he'll be off the premises, through the door down the steps and barred for life."

"You'll be doing the community a serious disservice if you do that, sir."

"It's my pub, used by basically good and honest folk out to have a relaxing couple of hours from the rigours of life, not for the use of a police informant, listening and prying into everyone's conversation and affairs."

However, the bottle-snatching raid never material-ized. A death in the gang-leader's family put paid to that, and it was called off. And Eddie, as pleased as punch, could visualize Welsby's frustration and anger at a missed opportunity to save a gang of desperate kids from a life of villainy

The pub was doing well. Trade was good. The Three Crowns Darters were top of the league. Their captain, Ethel Black, was now leading them to regular wins in other pubs that had also taken up the challenge of forming a ladies darts team.

And what with Sid, the pianist, fag dangling from his lips, banging out all the favourite melodious singsongs, whilst visiting artistes quaffed a refreshing half-time drink, Eddie and Ethel were a couple of happy landlords.

Now well established, and with his future seemingly secure, Eddie began to consider how to improve his existing staffing arrangements. After all, Ethel was now spending more time throwing darts than behind the bar serving drinks. And with this in mind, he approached Michael "Mick" Cranford, a middle-aged widower who lived with his only son, John, further along Mayflower Road.

Mick's low-profile manner had always been taken for granted: quiet, unassuming and yet diligently helpful in a slow, plodding way, clearing away glasses, wiping table tops, mopping spilled beer and even serving the odd pint to thirsty customers playing darts or dominoes, all without pay, but with an understanding that all of his drinks were free.

"How about a regular paid job and an apron thrown in, Mick?" Eddie said one Sunday night.

For a moment, Mick looked nonplussed, but as the friendly offer sank in, he became agitated and, for some reason, embarrassed and tetchy.

"Why should I, Eddie. I like things as they are, doing things in my own sweet way, nice and steady, like."

"But you've earned it. I don't want you to change your ways, just to get some benefit from what you're already doing for nowt. Ethel and me trust and respect you, Mick; you're like one of the family."

Mick became unreasonable.

"I don't want your bloody job, and I don't want your trust . . . and you know what you can do with your bloody money . . . I'm off!"

And before Eddie could draw breath, Mick walked out, slamming the door as he went.

"What was all that about?" Ethel said.

"You tell me. I've just offered an out-of-work widower a permanent paid position that he was already doing for nowt, and he's walked off in disgust." He scratched his head. "As the saying goes, 'There's nowt as queer as folk'."

The following day, halfway through the task of cleaning his beer pumps, Eddie had an unexpected visitor.

"I've come to apologise and explain away Dad's little upsetting," John Cranford said.

"It'll have to be good."

"You put him on a spot last night, Eddie. You made him feel right guilty with that offer of yours."

"Guilty?"

"Dad is Welsby's informer."

Once again, Eddie was knocked sideways.

"You see, Welsby caught me red-handed nickin' coal from t' sidings and promised to take no action if I could persuade Dad to do some listening in while clearing the tables and suchlike."

"The lousy swine!"

"I'm sorry, Eddie. All this trouble is my fault. I've dragged Dad down with me, and now he's had it with you too."

"Forget what's happened. Just tell your dad to be here, 8 o'clock sharp tonight, and there'll be a brand new apron waiting for him and a bottle o' milk stout . . . But for goodness sake, tell him to leave his listening ears at home."

"But what about Welsby?"

"Let me do some thinking about him."

It was the month of December, a bitterly cold December, too, when Eddie Black put his thinking into a plan of action.

Over tea and biscuits in the pub's living quarters, Eddie outlined his scheme to an attentive Mick and John.

"From what I've gathered since coming here, there's more coal nicked in December than any other time of the year, is that right?"

"That's true," John said. "It's usually the onset of really cold weather that does it. Christmas is just around the corner, and, besides keeping us warm, plenty make a bob or two selling the stuff."

"So some of the locals will be out in force, eh?"

"That's for sure."

"Well, how about choosing one particular night to carry out two raids. Two coal raids in one night and inform Welsby when it's going to be."

"Now, just a minute . . ."

"Revenge," Eddie said. He looked first at Mick and then at John and smiled a wicked smile. "The revenge of the stool pigeon."

"I don't follow," Mick said.

"Right, this is the plan. John will spread the word that no one, but no one, must go anywhere near the sidings on the night in question."

"I'm still not with you."

"Right. We choose a night to carry out two raids. Welsby will be informed about the raids, but they won't be carried out. Ironically, the railway will be out of bounds to everyone except the cops."

"It'll never work," John said.

Eddie ignored him and took down a calendar from the living-room wall.

"How about next Sunday, then? John, you spread the word there will be no coal nicking next Sunday night. You, Mick, and this will be your last stool-pigeon job, you get word to Welsby that there will be two raids on that particular night."

"Two? Are you sure about this?"

"Two. One about 8 o'clock, and the other after midnight."

"But won't he get suspicious when nobody turns up for the first one?"

"Why should he? We all know Sergeant Welsby, as keen as mustard, a Mountie always gets his man, that sort of thing. Even if nobody turns up for the 8 o'clock one, which they won't, he's certain to hang on and wait for the next one. Don't you think so?"

"I'm sure so," said John.

"So we all know what the plan is?"

"I spread the word, definitely no thieving any coal next Sunday night," John said.

"And I inform Welsby there will be two raids next Sunday night, one at 8 o'clock and another after midnight," Mick said.

"Brilliant," Eddie said.

And that's how officer Welsby got his comeuppance. He, a constable and two railway police, lay in wait for two raids that never happened. And just to put the icing on the cake (so to speak), on one of the coldest December nights on record, it began to snow, and Welsby, chilled to the marrow, caught pneumonia and was confined to his bed for three frustrating weeks, compliments of a stool pigeon's revenge.

John "10'

"Do You Remember?"
A True Character

"DO YOU REMEMBER?"

How many times have I written those words, "Do You Remember?" Quite a few by all accounts.

But by remembering I am constantly reminded of certain incidents, places and characters. Now what are the ingredients that make a true character? Is it eccentricity? Eccentrics strive to be eccentric. Some dress bizarrely just to draw attention to themselves. Some take pains to act bizarrely. Some take on extraordinary hobbies. All these methods are meant to attract. Contrivance is their sole aim in life.

Now a true character isn't weird or bizarre or grotesque. The true character is distinguished by an easy, unaffected way that singles him (or her) out from the rest of us. He's outstanding without any affectation. He can turn a drama into a comedy. A comedy into a drama. He won't be too gregarious. He knows his own mind. He knows his own strengths and weaknesses. He is unorganized, unconventional and unorthodox. He has a certain way that people around him find impulsively attracting.

These characteristics seemed much more plentiful in those early days of want and little waste. I truly believe that circumstances and conditions bring out the best in people. It proved to be so in those years of strife. It proved to be so in the war years. And even in our modern times, it has proved to be so.

Those, now, often climate disasters and unlawful disturbances bring out the best in our society. On the other hand, the brutality and viciousness that are now a familiar part of our lives should never be seen as characteristically right. Violence is wrong, and anything or anybody that promotes violence should be shunned.

One of the most outstanding characters that I ever knew was a man of God. A Roman Catholic priest. Father Rimmer was the most ardent priest that ever served the God-fearing parishioners of St Joseph's Catholic church. His sermons were loud and fearsome. Everyone came away from one of his sermons knowing that he knew their most inner, sinful thoughts. And his collections would have made Robin Hood blush. With his collection bag at the ready, his knock and enter methods were swift and breathtaking, and always followed by a grateful cup of tea, biscuits and a well-earned fag.

And God help (literally) any young Catholic man or woman who began a courtship with a non-Catholic. His methods of detection were incredible to say the least, and there was only one escape route. Leave the country.

Now, he was a genuine, true character. One to fear and one to respect. And one to remember.

"DO YOU REMEMBER?"

CHAPTER
ELEVEN

Mam and Dad:
and Another World

Some great thinkers reckon that one's life has already been plotted, planned and determined whilst still in the womb. I'm not so sure, but what I do know, without a shadow of a doubt, is that my Dad is solely responsible for every word I have ever written about my early life, not far from Wigan Pier.

Don't misunderstand me; he didn't encourage or inspire me. No way. Actually, it was all down to something he didn't do. He didn't die in 1918 when a German bullet missed his windpipe by a hair's breadth.

And years later, he didn't move house. Mam was keen on the idea, but Dad resisted, and in doing so, it was left to me, pencil poised, to put the period, the people and the place into print before all was lost in the hazy mists of time.

My dad, Thomas Dakin, was born in a canal cottage at Spencer's Bridge, near the village of Newburgh, approximately seven miles from Wigan, on the 24th March 1899.

On May 10th, 1917, Dad enlisted to fight in The Great War; he had just turned eighteen. He became a private in the Welsh Fusiliers and, after a few months training, was shipped out to France.

On their first day on foreign soil, the regiment was transported by London buses up to the frontline. He and his company were detailed to flushout a company of German soldiers who were holed-up in a small wood near the village of Estéres. They managed to get to within three hundred yards of the copse; but the enemy, possessing heavy artillery, began an almighty bombardment. However, the British "dug in" and managed to hold their positions.

In the fierce battle that followed, many British soldiers threw down their arms and began to retreat. Their commanding officer drew his revolver and threatened to shoot anyone who refused to hold his position. Eventually, the troops returned to their post, and order was restored.

After another few yards' advance, Dad and a few of his mates were pinned down again. This time they were trapped in a dip in a nearby field. For better protection they dug shallow trenches with their bayonets.

In the chaos that followed, they became separated from the rest of the party. As light began to fade, Dad and a few more managed to reach an isolated farm owned by two old women. The farm was already occupied by a squad of Welsh Guards who were awaiting orders to attack the German-held wood. Dad, who at one point was concealed behind a tree, managed to "down" a German soldier who was part of a group trying to reach his comrades in the wood.

Some time later, with supplies running low, Dad volunteered to fetch water from the farmhouse well. As he was crossing the yard, he was caught in a hail of bullets fired from the copse. A machine-gun bullet entered his neck a few inches below his left ear, and down he went. The time was about 3a.m. on Sunday 13th May, 1918. He was unconscious for some time and came to with blood pumping from his mouth and a shadowy figure kneeling over him. Later that morning, he was taken by a London bus, with other wounded, to safety behind the lines.

He was shipped from France and hospitalized at Birkenhead, near Liverpool. The bullet, which was lodged in his *right* shoulder (on the opposite side of entry), was found by a matron and duly removed. It had missed his wind-pipe by a mere fraction. Because of his injuries he couldn't speak for three months. They gave him the bullet as a memento of his brush with death.

Whilst recovering, he and other injured troops were entertained nightly in a large marquee.

Dad became friendly with a soldier suffering from the effects of shellshock; he stole the man's army greatcoat to replace the one he had lost in France.

While recuperating, he met a Doctor Floydd, a retired GP, who used to have a panel of wealthy patients. Apparently, he was a very generous person and supplied Dad and other casualties with food and cigarettes. He owned a large house and kept photographs of all the soldiers he had befriended on the walls of his living room.

Dad would run errands for the hospital staff and the less fortunate victims of war, using local trams or walking. They (the wounded) were well treated. If they were wearing hospital-blue, transport, cafes and theatres were all free.

After serving a total of one year and 170 days, Dad was finally discharged on January 14th, 1919. He returned home wearing a thin, cheap demob suit, and with a war pension of seven shillings and sixpence a week, which, when he was on the dole, he relinquished for a lump sum of £10.

On Dad's discharge certificate are the following words:

BEING SURPLUS TO MILITARY
REQUIREMENTS
(HAVING SUFFERED IMPAIRMENT SINCE
ENTRY INTO SERVICE)

He received one blue stripe for the wound inflicted.

Thomas Dakin met Frances Leach in 1921. At that time, Tom was labouring in a small brickyard in Hindley, a sub-district of Wigan, and Frances was employed at the same place as a clerk.

Frances, and her three sisters, Agnes, Annie and Nellie, were Hindley residents. Their parents, Richard and Bridget, ran Low Hall Farm, but Frances, having done quite enough farming as a girl, decided to move on and see what the other side of a cow looked like, and found Tom.

Tom too, was a rural man. His parents, Richard and Margaret, worked a narrow boat on the Leeds-Liverpool canal and were canal folk, born and bred. Indeed, Richard was born on a canal boat at Bottom Locks, Runcorn, Cheshire.

But with the advent of the steam engine and a dramatic improvement in road transportation, plus a few domestic problems, my future grandparents decided to sell up and settle down in Wigan.

And that's it. Not much of a high-flying start for my future parents, but there you have it.

Two people, both rural bred, destined by circumstances beyond their control, meet amongst a romantic setting of newly-baked house bricks, with fast-beating hearts, racing pulses and sweaty palms. And one year later a commitment of undying love and trust.

The marriage was solemnized at St. Benedict's Catholic church, Market Street, Hindley, on 20th May, 1922, and on that day, Dad, who was a protestant, crossed over and became a Roman Catholic for life. And a devout one, too.

And for me that showed a strength of character (and love), because in those early days a change of one's religion of this kind was frowned upon and never really accepted, especially by some family members and local communities.

And the community they chose to live in was not far from Wigan Pier. A humble, rented terraced house just around the corner from Dad's parents, with their very own water closet 40 yards from the back door, at the top end of a communal yard. And just to give the area a touch of class and palatial sumptuousness, a boneworks 300 yards from their front door, who, just to prove they were still in business and fully productive, released an invisible, but extremely obnoxious, detectable stench into the surrounding houses, shops and pubs and up wrinkled noses, as the local inhabitants tried in vain not to breathe in the deadly odour.

And just to make the situation even better, Dad, after spending many months on the dole, managed to get a job there, a job that lasted quite a while and even I, the youngest of the brood, can still remember Dad as a walking stink bomb.

Mam's three sisters had done much better in the marriage stakes. Their husbands, although far from wealthy, had never even seen a dole queue, but were still much better off financially.

Auntie Annie's husband was a farm manager in Shevington, a little hamlet not far from Wigan, and in desperate, penurious times, Auntie Annie would visit our crumbling paradise laden with baskets of food for a grateful sister and her hungry tribe of patched-up kids.

It was on one of these mercy trips that Auntie Annie gave Mam the idea of moving house. Apparently, a house in the village, not far from the farm, had become vacant. And what could be better than raising a family in such an environment? A classy rural village surrounded by verdant fields and woods, free from grime and pungent odours? It took some time and a lot of talking to persuade Dad, though. What about his job at the boneworks? What about schooling for the kids? Could they afford the rent? What sort of neighbours would they have? As strangers, would they be accepted into their way of life?

Anyhow, with time and patience, Mam finally won him over. Her convincing and determination left him no choice but to agree.

The landlady, Miss Ballard was informed; a date for the flit was arranged. And silence reigned. Dad hardly spoke a word. He became morose and, unusual for him, bad tempered. Times were tense. Then, two days before the set date, and still with a few pitiful odds and sods to pack, Dad, master of all he surveyed, reneged. He wouldn't budge. There was too much at stake. The future too uncertain. We were staying put! And that was that!

Our very irate landlady was hurriedly informed. Her plans for a new tenant had to be hastily abandoned, and Mam, although exasperated and disappointed, gave a deep sigh of relief as life, such as it was, returned to normality.

But normality never lasts for long, does it? After years working the waterways, my paternal grandparents were finding it hard to settle down. But luckily for Granddad, the house boasted a small allotment at the rear, and he spent his time among chickens, rhubarb and lettuce. However, a few occasional boozing sessions saw him lose his direction a little. Like the time he tried to sell certain family heirlooms down at the pub.

But apart from these interludes of madness, he always seemed to be working: hammering, sawing, digging, tarring coops and sheds and whitewashing walls. And no one in our family, including myself, escaped these endless, laborious chores. Aye, pay him a visit, and you ended up with blisters on your hands, and no thanks to follow.

Uniquely, he could be both cruel and kind. An ailing chicken was placed in a well-padded basket near the open coal fire and hand-fed until fully recovered. And yet again if a chicken was required for the Sunday table, he'd choose his victim, shove the bird between his bony knees, and, with me or one of my brothers gripping its horny, kicking claws at his rear, he would pierce and probe like an amateur surgeon with his penknife, until the carotid artery was found and severed, then still twitching convulsively, the animal was hung up to drip-dry.

Granddad, although he enjoyed an occasional few glasses of beer, was a cold and austere man, but I shall always remember him for the compassion shown to a poorly chicken and his penchant for wearing a small, knitted, black skullcap in his sickbed. And it was on this same bed that Dad and Uncle Dick, one of Dad's brothers, washed his lifeless body in preparation for his last journey to that great and winding waterway in the sky.

164

Grandma Dakin outlived her husband by many years, but, for a while it looked like it wasn't meant to be.

Shortly after Granddad's demise, Grandma, too, became gravely ill. A doctor was urgently summonsed, and he in turn, informed Mam to prepare for the worst.

"She won't last the night, I'm afraid," he said, solemnly.

He obviously didn't know how tough Grandma really was. The old lady lived on for many years before finally meeting her maker.

But over the years, it was Mam who really suffered. Living in close proximity to her aged in-laws, she became the only true and trustworthy link between their restricted lifestyle and the outside world.

Neither of these water gypsies could read or write, and, as their years advanced and their health deteriorated, they relied more and more on Mam's ability to nurse, clean, shop and cook. In an age when domestic appliances (hoovers, washers and electric irons) were virtually non-existent (and taking in washing, as well), Mam's day to day survival was an endless, thankless struggle.

For a woman who had been raised on a family farm by conscientious, even-tempered, farming parents to end up slaving for one and all, day in day out, the thought of that missed opportunity to enjoy the tranquillity of Shevington village, must have caused some bitter, inner anguish.

I never really knew my maternal grandparents. My sister, Kathleen, went on regular visits, but I only once.

Low Hall Farm was surprisingly close to the Hindley's main thoroughfare. A reasonable walk from the bus stop, and you were there. I don't remember much of my visit really. I don't remember any greeting, no hugs and kisses or even having anything to eat. But I suppose I must have.

What I do remember is having this sudden urge to use the toilet and being escorted to this ramshackle, wooden outbuilding, with a very precarious, deep, wooden-lidded, "bombs away!", faecal cesspit that functioned as an outside lavatory. Clutching the sides fearfully, I had the fastest "number two" of my entire life and hurried back indoors, never to return.

What are the ingredients for a stable, happy marriage? Wealth? Dedication? Love? Tolerance? Or is it a combination of all these?

Who knows for sure?

Mam and Dad had five kids: Kathleen, Thomas, John and me, Edward, and in that order, and somewhere along the way, they lost a baby girl, Mary.

Like most wives in those desperate times, Mam was the one who suffered most. Her working day, every day, was drudgery. She toiled slavishly from morning till night. For a woman dedicated to the needs of her family, this meant she had very little time to herself. I never saw her settle down and read

166

a book, use lipstick, rouge or perfume, but I often did see her knitting, sewing, crocheting and patching, all done to ease the family burden of having nowt. She was slavishly tolerant to the hardships of penurious motherhood and gave us and Dad as much comfort and support as she possibly could from a dire family income.

But even with a lack of cash, she was never submissive. Like the time Dad was on the dole. Someone advised her to apply for a little extra State Welfare money. This meant a visit to the workhouse to face a panel of inquisitors.

"No way," she said. "We'll manage somehow."

But things got worse, so Dad went instead. They eventually gave them an extra five shillings a week. With this and some extra washing she took in, that included bloodstained butcher's aprons, the burden became a little easier. She washed Mondays and Tuesdays and ironed on Wednesdays. At that time, her smoothing iron was a gas operated one. I can see her now, climbing first on a chair, then onto our solid, square dinner table in the centre of the living room, removing the gas-mantle and connecting a tube from the fitting down to the iron itself. Close to the gas-fitting there was a suspended two-pole clothes horse attached to the ceiling, from which she hung her bedclothes. This too, could only be reached by standing on the table.

Many years later, a cousin of hers, a joiner, sawed the thing off close to the ceiling and fixed the two poles on a rope pulley that could be lowered and raised with ease. Technology, eh!

Mam was the pivot, the centre of all that was essential to our childhood. Always doing. Our house may have been a rented (four shillings and sixpence a week) one, but she made it hers. Scantily furnished, it may have been, with odd square pieces of carpet on the floor and a black-leaded fire range that was our only source of heat and newly baked bread, but she polished, black leaded and beat those carpets relentlessly, until the place smelt and shone like a country mansion.

God knows how she found time for visitors, but she did, and always with a welcoming cup of tea and a slice of her homemade cake.

It was always Mam who went without, and we, the family, Dad and all, never appreciated her love and dedication and tolerance, until it was too late. We never kissed or hugged her and never said, "Thanks Mam". But deep down, we loved her, and in later years we came to realize and appreciate how unselfishly she had given her very life to us, her family.

So, where does that leave Dad. To be brutally honest, left on his own, Dad wouldn't have lasted a week. Oh, he was honest and trustworthy and (given the chance) a reliable family provider, handing over a labourer's wage or a week's dole money, whatever was available at the time. But he never did any household chores. He never dusted, polished or cooked. I don't think I ever saw him make a cup of tea, even. But he decorated (using colour wash) and soled and heeled our shoes, renewed the irons on our clogs and cut our hair. He never hit us. Mam did all the clouting at our house. But Dad was still a force to be reckoned with. One look from him was sufficient enough to deter any roistering or indiscipline from his unruly brood.

Dad was never one for standing on street corners, gossiping. He was friendly enough and would stop and talk about this and that and t'other, but never make it his business to stand under the gas lamp and join in with the rest.

Dad believed absolutely in physical exercise. Walking and gathering herbs was his favourite pastime. And, much to Mam's chagrin, he also became addicted to the more strenuous kind of exercise.

For years (in the better times), Dad spent precious household money on a variety of body building courses, all claiming to improve the human body to a degree of fitness and muscularity never before achieved: Benjamin Borroughs' Indian Club Swinging course (including a pair of heavy, highly polished, wooden clubs) guaranteed to improve the upper body and strengthen the heart; T. W. Standwell, a magnificent, moustached individual, whose deep breathing, free-standing, exercises and early morning cold water "tubs" would improve the lungs, circulation, heart, digestion and confidence; Charles Atlas — "Have a body like mine" — with many sepia coloured photographs of him doing press-ups and a variety of muscle dynamics; and, last but not least, Alfred Danks, another fantastically muscular specimen, who claimed that anyone who followed his chest expander routine (beautifully illustrated by Danks himself on a large black and white wall chart), could attain a similar physique by the use of his own brand of expander.

Then, of course there was the "inner man" to take care of: chlorophyll tablets for the blood; Elasto "walk right" circulation tablets; stomach potions. If they were meant to cure or do good, Dad was having a go.

I suppose Mam must have ranted and raved at such wilful waste, but I never heard her. Like all married couples, they must have had their differences, especially about money (or lack of it). But I only ever heard them quarrel once, and that was over something trivial.

Mam and Dad weren't exactly compatible, but their relationship worked. They were tolerant of each other, especially Mam with Dad. She gave her mind, body and soul to the raising of her family. Dad did his share, with reservations, but at the same time, he was an essential cog in our family life. A man who we respected and whom we could rely on to help Mam along that uncertain road into the future.

I was born 23rd March, 1931. The youngest of four. I was three years old before I could talk, which convinced my paternal grandma (or so I'm told) to often comment, "Thall never raise that child, Frances."

When I reached the age of five, my sister, Kathleen, walked me to the Dickensian Catholic school of St

Joseph's for my very first day of schooling, where I promptly kicked Sister Maria (a teaching nun) in the shins.

The school didn't have mixed classes. I don't know about the girls, but on the boys' side, the teachers (and this includes the female ones) ruled with fist and cane. Absence for any reason, sickness, a death in the family, anything, would not be tolerated.

The school, as I remember, didn't teach physical education (among other things). PE at our school meant Premature Ejaculation.

Their teaching methods were pathetic, to say the least. Luckily for me, my sister, Kathleen, taught me to read and write. But some pupils weren't so fortunate and left school without any educational qualifications of any kind. For them, reading and writing and mathematics were still as much a mystery on leaving school as when they started. Indeed, one ex-classmate, who I happened to meet at my first army training camp, still couldn't read or write, and, until the army took steps to remedy this, I, his only link with home, read and wrote all of his personal correspondence.

From a male point of view, there was only one way to escape the cruel attentions of St Joseph's sadist teachers. Be part of a rugby team, and go to church several times a week. Do this, and leniency (if not popularity) was assured.

Leaving school at 14 was akin to leaving prison, but better. And, with the expectations of a new life of pick and choose, I was ecstatic. Not for long, though.

Although the only woodwork I had ever handled at school had been my desk lid, I had this feeling for carpentry. But it wasn't to be. Dole visits. Walking the streets. Scanning job adverts, all came to nothing. Perhaps the invention of plastic and Bakelite was the reason!

Mam and Dad, too, were getting a little impatient. They weren't bothered about my enthusiastic outlook; they wanted me off the streets and in work, any work. Like the majority of hard-up parents in that day and age, it was money they wanted, not a jobless, trade-seeking son.

It was eagle-eyed Dad who saw it first. It was one Friday evening, just after tea. He opened his paper, like he always did, went straight to the job vacancies page and with a tremor in his voice, read his findings aloud to an attentive mother and a disillusioned son.

A week later, I was in the leather trade. Dad's fantastic find with fantastic opportunities was with a small saddler's business near the town centre. I hated it! A hate that never diminished right up to handing in my notice to quit, two long years later.

I was then shunted into dairy work. Another lousy job, and when the foreman demanded that I work overtime cleaning a milk sterilizing machine, I took the opportunity to pack that job in too.

My troubles now became twofold. Finding work had now become almost impossible. I had just turned 17, and in a few months' time, the War Office would be chasing me. So, with no job on the horizon and the armed forces waiting in the wings, it was a desperate situation. And Mam and Dad weren't very pleased, either.

A dole clerk solved the problem. A cotton factory, Trencherfield Mill, was in need of a "beam-dropper" labourer in their winding room; so, with little hope of success, I went along. Their needs must have been as desperate as the Dakin family. Overlooking my pending National Service call-up, they gave me the job.

A beam-dropping job is active, fairly arduous, but simple to do. An empty cotton beam, which is actually a five foot long bobbin, is hooked onto a chain-pulley and ratcheted up to waist level, pushed along on an overhead track to a waiting lady-winder, transferred to her winding machine to replace a cotton-filled one, which was pushed back along the overhead runner to a loading bay to await collection.

It was an enjoyable job, really. Surrounded by hot, sweaty and often randy females, wearing very little clothing, the effects on a 17-year-old virgin could be erotically stimulating.

But my wandering eye came to an abrupt stop early one Monday morning. She had long auburn hair, blue eyes and a bonny face, which that day, was looking rather flushed with the hustle and bustle of being late for work. Charlie, the foreman, gave her his last verbal warning before she hurried away to her machine.

But I was smitten. Why had it happened now? Why had I never noticed before how good-looking and desirable she was? Why did I keep getting this odd feeling in my stomach? Two days later, I asked her out. She, much to my surprise, accepted. Within weeks, it was love.

We spent nights at the pictures. Days (weekends and holidays) biking around the rural parts of Wigan, and our mutual love grew stronger by the day.

About three weeks before my call-up, Eileen began to experience lengthy spells of tiredness. Her fresh complexion was replaced by two unusual, permanent, flush-red cheeks, and a disturbing, intermittent cough. She was soon diagnosed as having tuberculosis.

As I was on my way to my first army barracks, Eileen was being admitted to a TB hospital.

We wrote almost daily, and the knowledge of her illness only made my introduction to the strange, disciplinary life of the military all the more traumatic and unsettling, especially when I received word to say she was now coughing up a little blood.

But army life didn't give me much time to dwell on the sentimental issues of my private life. And time marched on (so to speak). On my infrequent leaves from duty, I spent time visiting Eileen in hospital and drowning my sorrows with mates still in civvy street.

Two years later, just prior to my demob, Eileen too, was released from hospital. She hadn't responded to treatment. Streptomycin and other treatments had failed utterly. She took to her bed and began a slow decline to the inevitable. She died in January, 1952.

Three weeks after my demob, I returned to Trencherfield Mill, but the memories were too painful and poignant. I handed in my notice, and once again I joined that never-ending dole queue.

It was a chap with the unflattering nickname "The Skull" who found me work.

Ernie "The Skull" Lowry was a chain-smoking lazy sod of a neighbour, whose hairless pate shone like a white beacon in the dark and who spent most of his time (and money) in the company of Jack Dash, the bookie's runner, betting on the gee-gees, as he called them.

We met in the dole queue. He suggested (with a puff of smoke) that we try our luck at the then corporation water department, from where, in fact, he had been sacked earlier that same year.

That chance meeting and that chance suggestion was to change my life for ever.

I was taken on and employed as a labourer digging trenches for water mains and from this lowest of positions, made an unhurried, fortunate and conscientious climb to management status.

And The Skull? Well, he, too was hired, but was soon given the boot for spending too much time leaning on his spade with a fag in his mouth.

I often wish I could be transported back to that other world. To those distant days when cotton-covered, clog-shod mill girls thronged our cobbled streets. When dust-caked miners hurried home to their tin baths. To meet, once again, those friends, neighbours and relatives of an unforgettable age. Back to a time when decency, and discipline, honour and respect for parents, other people and property, was the norm. Back to a gentler age before progress and technology brought in the bulldozers to obliterate a whole community (our boneworks; our brickyard: our sand hills; our houses and our way of life) and left us teetering on the brink of uncertainty.

But those machines of destruction couldn't bulldoze away our memories. They will live on as long as there is someone left to remember, and, in remembering, will bring the past forward and into the future

Also available in ISIS Large Print:

Wicksy and the King's Shilling

Peter Wicks

"I lined the bed up and simply dropped it. The divan legs dropped over neatly, and he was pinned.
'You've forgotten your bed!' I said loudly as I added my fourteen stone weight to the snare."

Peter Wicks dedicates the third instalment of his memoirs to his father, Frank Wicks, who fought in the trenches of the First World War. Now in his teens, Peter receives his own conscription papers, destined to become a military policeman. During his training, he learnt to drive and discovered that bullies will be found in all walks of life. This book follows Peter's military career from training to demobilisation.

Included is also Peter's poem "The Return" written in response to Wilfred Owen's "The Send Off".

ISBN 978-0-7531-5273-7 (hb)
ISBN 978-0-7531-5274-4 (pb)

A 1950s Childhood

Paul Feeney

"No, you haven't really got the latest six-shooter cap-gun with matching holsters, but you've seen one in your local Woolworths store and you dream of having it, along with all the other trappings of your big-screen cowboy heroes."

Do you remember Pathé News? The purple stains of iodine on the knees of boys in short trousers? Knitted bathing costumes? Then the chances are you were born in or around 1950. Today the 1950s seems like another age. But for those born around then, this era seems like yesterday. From waking up to ice on the inside of the windows, washing in a tin bath by the fire and spoonfuls of cod-liver oil, life was very different to today. This delightful compendium of memories will appeal to all who grew up in this post-war decade, whether in town or country, wealth or poverty.

ISBN 978-0-7531-5271-3 (hb)
ISBN 978-0-7531-5272-0 (pb)

The Scent of the Countryside

Doris E. Gawrys

"I soon found Smut a very willing 'baby'. I dressed him in my doll's clothes, wrapped him in a shawl and put him in my doll's pram. Then off we would go for a walk. He actually seemed to enjoy it and never made any attempt to escape from me, or the pram — I know everyone was surprised and amused that my 'doll' was a black cat."

Doris Gawrys has such fond memories of her childhood home that she dedicates this memoir to the house "Pengelly" in Rayleigh, Essex. With its white roses by the door, working well and dragonfly ponds, Pengelly was a playground for Doris, her cousin Mollie and brother Bobby, who was born in the house. Though still very young when the family moved again she has never forgotten those days.

ISBN 978-0-7531-9592-5 (hb)
ISBN 978-0-7531-9593-2 (pb)

Wigan Pier Goodbye

Ted Dakin

"My escape from a school that taught me very little was a euphoric occasion and because of the headmaster's ruling that only short pants should be worn by all pupils, my first pair of long ones was an added bonus."

Ted Dakin returns to his childhood in Wigan, with more stories of the people and places he grew up with. He tells of boxing matches ruled over by his vindictive headmaster, Owd Hector Wainwright; of men stealing coal from the trains; and of his first job in a saddlery. Full of the characters of his youth, like Dolly Varden and her predictions, Fag-Ash Lil and Dunkirk veteran Ginger Dyson, Ted's stories are full of the warmth and wit of a Wigan lad.

ISBN 978-0-7531-9510-9 (hb)
ISBN 978-0-7531-9511-6 (pb)